3-MINUTE PRAYERS

FOR GUYS

JUSTIN

Published by Barbour Books, an imprint of Barbour Publishing, Inc., 1810 Barbour Drive, Uhrichsville, Ohio 44683, www.barbourbooks.com

Our mission is to inspire the world with the life-changing message of the Bible.

Member of the
Evangelical Christian
Publishers Association

Printed in the United States of America.

3-MINUTE PRAYERS
FOR GUYS

Glenn Hascall

BARBOUR BOOKS
An Imprint of Barbour Publishing, Inc.

INTRODUCTION

Pray continually.
1 THESSALONIANS 5:17

These timely, inspiring prayers are written especially for guys, teenagers for whom a solid foundation of scripture and prayer will help them weather the storms of life. Guys, just three minutes is all you'll need to charge your spiritual batteries for the busy, happy, scary, or exciting things you'll face each day:

- Minute 1: Read and reflect on God's Word.
- Minute 2: Pray, using the provided prayer to jump-start a conversation with God.
- Minute 3: Reflect on a question or two for further thought.

This book isn't meant to replace your own Bible reading and study. But every one of these scriptures and prayers can help keep you grounded—focused on the One who hears all your prayers. May this book remind you that the heavenly Father cares about everything you have to say. So go on. . .talk to Him today. He's ready and waiting to hear from you!

DIFFERENT THAN YOU

"God is not human, that he should lie, not a human being, that he should change his mind. Does he speak and then not act? Does he promise and not fulfill?"
NUMBERS 23:19

Lord, You are not like anyone I know. You're different. You always tell the truth and You never change Your mind. When You say something, You mean it. When You make a promise, You keep it. I can't compare You to any person I know because You beat them in every category. You are stronger and wiser, and Your plans are always better. You're with me when no one else wants to be. May I remember to respect the differences between You and everyone else I will ever know. Help me follow You as the Truth Teller, the Confident One, and the Promise Keeper.

THINK ABOUT IT

In what ways do you think of God as "different" than you? The same? Why is it important to become more like Him instead of God becoming more like you?

THE WORLD

*In the beginning God created
the heaven and the earth.*
GENESIS 1:1 KJV

Dear God, there was a time when this world came into being. You get the credit. You created every mountain, valley, river, flower, and tree for me to enjoy. The oceans, fish, whales, and coral reefs demonstrate Your creativity and order. And this planet is the home for mankind. You made sure it could meet my needs. I have air, water, and food because You made them and keep them, and You give people the wisdom to manage them. No one can take credit for this planet but You. No one can create a sunset but You. No one can create such incredible diversity in nature but You. Help me to appreciate all that You have created, to show gratitude for all the things You've made for me to enjoy.

THINK ABOUT IT

*Is it important to believe that God created
the world? Why or why not? What part of
nature causes you to worship God?*

THE MARK WAS MISSED

*All have sinned and fall short of the glory of God,
and are justified by his grace as a gift, through
the redemption that is in Christ Jesus.*
ROMANS 3:23–24 ESV

Lord, there is nothing I can do to make up for failing You. One sin removes me from Your list of perfect people. You said that everyone falls short. But You also said I am made right by Your grace. You called grace a gift, and You said I need to accept it. When Jesus died on the cross, He was saving me from a guilty verdict. Jesus made it possible for me to be pure in Your eyes because He is pure in Your eyes. What I can't do, Jesus already did. What I need most is what Jesus has already offered. What I want is to be Your friend.

THINK ABOUT IT

*How have you tried to impress God?
Why do you think what God has done is
more important than what you have done?*

BROKEN. RESTORED.

There is a great difference between Adam's sin and God's gracious gift. For the sin of this one man, Adam, brought death to many. But even greater is God's wonderful grace and his gift of forgiveness to many through this other man, Jesus Christ. . . . For Adam's sin led to condemnation, but God's free gift leads to our being made right with God.
Romans 5:15–16 NLT

Dear God, You gave Adam one command and he broke it. You give me commands and I fail to obey. You knew I couldn't follow directions, so You made sure I could be made right through Your Son, Jesus Christ. Sin kills. Sin shortens life. Sin separates people. Maybe that's why You told me not to sin. Your forgiveness should motivate me to use Your strength to obey. You are willing to restore me. I'm grateful.

THINK ABOUT IT

How do you feel when You break God's law? How does it make you feel to know God can forgive your sin and restore your place in His family?

FRIENDSHIP INVITE

God demonstrates his own love for us in this:
While we were still sinners, Christ died for us.
ROMANS 5:8

Lord, You made people knowing that we would sin, and we all have. You made humanity knowing that we would never reach the goal of perfection, and we haven't. And You made human beings with a plan already in mind to save us from sin. The choices I make are like ropes that tie me up and limit my freedom. The gift of Your Son, Jesus, who died to pay the price for my sin, unties me and sets me free. This gift was the demonstration we needed to recognize that Your love was more than words. You didn't wait until we could become good enough. When we broke Your law, we became your enemy—but Your love asks me to be a friend.

THINK ABOUT IT

Why do you think God had to reach out to you first?
How does His gift demonstrate His love for you?

FAITHFUL AND JUST

*If we confess our sins, he is faithful and just to forgive us
our sins and to cleanse us from all unrighteousness.*
1 JOHN 1:9 ESV

God, I thank You for giving me a plan that leads to
life rescue. You have offered to forgive my sin and
make my record clean. That's the best offer I have
ever received. It's the best offer I have ever accepted.
Help me to recognize that I have broken your law.
Help me to understand that I'm wrong every time
I sin. When I'm honest, You forgive. When I accept
Your rescue, I'm welcomed as a member of Your
family. Thanks for being faithful in forgiving law-
breakers—me included. I want to be transformed. I
want to become more like You. I want what You want
for me. Help me to accept Your forgiveness and follow Your plan.

THINK ABOUT IT

*Why is it important for Jesus to forgive Your sin?
Why is it important to admit that You have broken
God's law? What is one benefit of being forgiven?*

THE ONE. THE ONLY.

Jesus answered, "I am the way and the truth and the life.
No one comes to the Father except through me."
JOHN 14:6

Dear God, Jesus said that He was the way, the truth, and the life. He said I can't come to You without going through Him. I keep hearing people say that there are many ways to You, many truths to consider, and that life is what I make it. But You tell me I can never really access the authentic life without Jesus. Your rescue for my life is Jesus, period—not Jesus and something else. He defines the way, the truth, and the real life. I can trust His truth, or I can try anything else on my own. But if there is no truth except Your truth, then anything else I believe is a lie.

THINK ABOUT IT

Why is it hard for some people to believe God offers the only way, truth, and life? Why is it important to believe Jesus is the only way, truth, and life?

TRUTH-SEEKING

All Scripture is inspired by God and is useful to teach us what is true and to make us realize what is wrong in our lives. It corrects us when we are wrong and teaches us to do what is right. God uses it to prepare and equip his people to do every good work.
2 TIMOTHY 3:16–17 NLT

Dear God, the words You authored are important for me to read. Thanks for making them instructions for my life. Thanks for giving me truth that doesn't change based on polls and popular opinions. It is safe to trust You because Your opinions never change. You never place amendments on truth. I can do what's right and avoid what's wrong when I actually know what You've said. You've given me a purpose, Lord—please make me ready to always do what will please You most.

THINK ABOUT IT

Why is it important that God decides what's true? Is it important to believe His truth even when others aren't convinced? Why?

PURITY

How can a young man keep his way pure? By guarding it according to your word. With my whole heart I seek you; let me not wander from your commandments!
<small>PSALM 119:9–10 ESV</small>

Dear God, thanks for reminding me that if I want my life to be recognized for purity, I need to read the Bible. Your words are like food to the hungry, water to the thirsty, and air to those who need oxygen. In other words, everybody. Life just won't make sense without Your wisdom. The more I know about who You are and the design You have for my life, the less confused I will be. If I treat my friendship with You like I'm trying to find something hidden, I'm not looking for the God who wants to be found. Let me follow You, learn from You, and agree that pursuing You will be the best adventure of my life.

THINK ABOUT IT

How can you keep your life pure?
Why do you think this is important to God?
Why should it be important to you?

TRANSFORMED

And so, dear brothers and sisters, I plead with you to give your bodies to God because of all he has done for you. Let them be a living and holy sacrifice—the kind he will find acceptable. This is truly the way to worship him. Don't copy the behavior and customs of this world, but let God transform you into a new person by changing the way you think. Then you will learn to know God's will for you, which is good and pleasing and perfect.

ROMANS 12:1–2 NLT

Lord, when I believed in Your Son, Jesus, You encouraged me to dedicate my body to You. Help me to care about how I treat it, what I put in it, and what I do with it. May I never use a clean page in my life story to copy what is considered normal by those who don't know You. Transform my thinking and actions so I can recognize Your plan for me.

THINK ABOUT IT

*In what ways can you dedicate your body,
life, and actions to God? How does
transformation appeal to you?*

GROWING SOMETHING GOOD

The fruit of the Spirit is love, joy, peace, forbearance,
kindness, goodness, faithfulness, gentleness and
self-control. Against such things there is no law.
GALATIANS 5:22–23

Dear God, You bring change to my life when I co-operate with Your Spirit. Your Spirit changes me. Hate is replaced by love, sorrow by joy, anxiety by peace, irritability by patience, insensitivity by kindness, dishonesty by goodness, disloyalty by faithfulness, cruelty by gentleness, and impulsiveness by self-control. There's no law against these transformations. They help me represent You. They help me see others as You do. May the fruit of Your spirit influence my life, encourage others to know You, and reflect Your character. You want to make changes in me. You want to make me a new creation. I want to welcome my new life in You.

THINK ABOUT IT

Do you think God wants you to access all
the fruit of His Spirit? Why or why not?
What aspects of life within the fruit of God's
Spirit do you struggle with most? Why?

IN STEP

*Those who belong to Christ Jesus have crucified the
flesh with its passions and desires. Since we live
by the Spirit, let us keep in step with the Spirit.*
GALATIANS 5:24–25

Lord, I am used to living my old life. The choices
I used to make are easy for me to make again. But
You say that when I accept new life from Your Son,
Jesus, I put the choices I once made in the grave.
Those choices no longer define who I am. The things
I used to want more than anything caused me to be
selfish and rude. My new choices can come through
the wisdom of Your Spirit. I can face new choices
with the companionship of Your Spirit. New choices
are a part of my new life, of the life I want to live.

THINK ABOUT IT

*Why do you think it is so easy to make choices
that don't reflect God's Spirit? Why should the
wisdom of God's Spirit make a difference
in the way you make choices?*

LOVE AUTHENTIC

Don't just pretend to love others. Really love them.
Hate what is wrong. Hold tightly to what is
good. Love each other with genuine affection,
and take delight in honoring each other.
ROMANS 12:9–10 NLT

Dear God, I know You want me to be real, transparent, and authentic. If I'm nice to someone but I don't really love them the way You want me to love them, I can expect them to see me as false. Fake love is like emotional sarcasm. My actions say I care, but something tells others I never really meant it. If I really care for others, let me not only be genuine, but also desire to honor them without trying to prove I'm in a compassion competition. Let me grip Your best plan and hold sin at arm's length. When I fail, bring me back to Your "help desk."

THINK ABOUT IT

How can you show genuine love to other
people? Why do you believe God sees love
as the most important command? How does
this love change your list of priorities?

RETHINK

Bless those who persecute you. Don't curse them; pray that God will bless them. Be happy with those who are happy, and weep with those who weep. Live in harmony with each other. Don't be too proud to enjoy the company of ordinary people. And don't think you know it all!
ROMANS 12:14–16 NLT

Father, I don't know why it's human nature to want someone to hurt when they hurt me, but You tell me to bless them, to pray that You will bless them, and to weep with my enemy. I'm supposed to live in harmony with people whose actions are off-key. I'm not supposed to pretend I know it all. I'm not supposed to act like I'm better than other people. To live with others even when they hurt others defines how a Christian should live, and I will need You to remind me of this. If no human beings are Your enemy, keep me from making them mine.

THINK ABOUT IT

Why do you think it's easy to think some people are worth your time while others are not? How can you live in harmony with others?

NO REAL ENEMY

If God is for us, who can be against us? He who did not spare his own Son but gave him up for us all, how will he not also with him graciously give us all things?
ROMANS 8:31–32 ESV

Lord, I have no real enemy, because You are my friend. You love me more than anyone could hate me. I know of Your love because long before I ever sinned, You sent Your Son, Jesus, to make sure we could remain friends beyond the moments when I would betray You. Every time I chose my way over Your command, I turned my back on You. Help me to always turn around and come back to You. I thank You for making that possible. My choices and Your commands are always at war. I need You to win that war. I want to obey. Your gifts are beyond measure. May I appreciate them more than I ever have before.

THINK ABOUT IT

Why is it important that God loves you more than anyone could hate you? What does it mean to you that God is for you

CREDIT DUE

*Sing out your thanks to the LORD; sing praises to
our God with a harp. He covers the heavens with
clouds, provides rain for the earth, and makes
the grass grow in mountain pastures.*
PSALM 147:7–8 NLT

Father, You made the heavens, the clouds, the rain,
the grass, and the mountains. I am told to proclaim
my thanks, and so I thank You. I know I am just a
part of Your creation, but You know me by name. You
loved me enough to provide a way for me to come
close to You when sin tries to keep me away from
You. Sometimes I can't do the things You want me
to do without help. Sometimes you send someone
along to help. Sometimes You help me personally.
And when I am the most honest, I will acknowledge
that I could never have done any good thing without
Your help. I am never alone.

THINK ABOUT IT

*Why should God get the credit for helping mankind?
Why should you be more interested in giving credit
to God than in claiming credit for yourself?*

CHANGED THINKING

Trust in the LORD with all your heart and lean not on your own understanding; in all your ways submit to him, and he will make your paths straight. Do not be wise in your own eyes; fear the LORD and shun evil.
PROVERBS 3:5–7 NIV

Dear God, today I'm learning new things—whether I like it or not. And if there are new things to learn, it makes sense to search for Your wisdom and rely less on my own opinion. I want to be thought of as an adult, and I hate to be proven wrong. But even now, at the moment I seek a ticket to adulthood, I need to remember that You know more than I ever will. You have answers when I'm busy only guessing. You can be trusted, when my choices make me untrustworthy, to make my path straight. Give me wisdom. Help me avoid sin.

THINK ABOUT IT

Why is it hard to search for God's wisdom in God's book? How should you respond when God's wisdom demands a change in thinking?

CRUSHED

*The LORD is near to the brokenhearted and saves
the crushed in spirit. Many are the afflictions of the
righteous, but the LORD delivers him out of them all.*
PSALM 34:18–19 ESV

Lord, there are days it seems like my emotions, my spirit, and my heart have become a punching bag. Your Word calls this being brokenhearted and crushed in spirit. It could be the things people say, the way I'm treated, or the betrayal of a friend. Help me remember that even when these days come, You've never left me. Even when the struggle is the hardest, You're working to rescue me from the pain I feel. I admit that I don't always understand why I feel the way I feel, and I don't always understand why people can be so cruel, but the pain I feel reminds me that You are my deliverer, healer, and restorer.

THINK ABOUT IT

*Why can it be difficult to turn to God the
moment you feel crushed and broken? When
is it the right time to trust that God will help?*

BE CAREFUL, LITTLE MOUTH

Understand this, my dear brothers and sisters:
You must all be quick to listen, slow to speak,
and slow to get angry. Human anger does not
produce the righteousness God desires.
JAMES 1:19–20 NLT

Dear God, there are days when it is all too easy to blow up emotionally. When I don't want to listen. When I can't stop talking. When the only way people can describe me is angry. You say that I can get angry, but I shouldn't commit that sin. When I get angry, I usually say things that hurt others. That's not loving—that's sin. I can count to ten before responding, or I can ask for Your help. I want to make a choice that pleases You. That's hard to do when my first response is anger. May Your love be the first thing that others see in the way I respond.

THINK ABOUT IT

Why is anger an easy first response?
Why does anger create so many problems?
If your goal is to be more like God, what
place should anger have in your relationships?

BEST THINKING

Finally, brothers and sisters, whatever is true, whatever is noble, whatever is right, whatever is pure, whatever is lovely, whatever is admirable—if anything is excellent or praiseworthy—think about such things.

PHILIPPIANS 4:8

Father, when I want proof that I'm on track in making decisions, help me remember that my decisions should look like Your truth. I should seek to make choices that are noble, right, pure, lovely, admirable, excellent, and praiseworthy. I should apply this test to the things I think as well as the things I do. Some things I make room for fail this test. Some choices I make are based on a lie. They lack nobility. They are wrong, impure, lacking love. They will never win Your applause. Help me shift my thinking. Help me find the blessing in Your plan for best thinking.

THINK ABOUT IT

How have recent choices you have made measured up to God's list? Does this list seem foolish? Why or why not? In what ways would your life reflect God's character if you followed this list?

KNOCK OFF ALL THAT FEARING

Fear not, for I am with you; be not dismayed, for I am your God; I will strengthen you, I will help you, I will uphold you with my righteous right hand.
ISAIAH 41:10 ESV

Lord, I know that worry is easy. Trust is much harder. It's easier to think about how bad things can get rather than think about how much You have blessed me. It's not tough to identify the complications of life, but it's hard to believe that Your answers can uncomplicate the difficult ones. I don't need to be troubled. I don't need to lose sleep. I don't need to face whatever I fear alone. You are with me, and You are God. When I am weak, You are strong. When I need help, You're on the way. But even though I read of Your power and willingness to help, I can still find myself anxious about things I can't control. In those moments, reassure me that You've got this.

THINK ABOUT IT

What are a few of the things You worry about most? How have these worries helped create a positive outcome?

TEMPTED, BUT NOT ALONE

The temptations in your life are no different
from what others experience. And God is faithful.
He will not allow the temptation to be more than
you can stand. When you are tempted, he will
show you a way out so that you can endure.
1 CORINTHIANS 10:13 NLT

Dear God, I know that temptations are urges to do things that break Your law. Temptations are also urges to give up doing things You say are important. It can be very easy to do the wrong thing, or fail to do the right thing, because I know You forgive. But You have a better way. You don't want me to say, "I can't do it." You want me to say, "The only way I can keep my distance from temptation is with Your help." It's good for me to remember I'm not alone. Everyone faces temptations. Everyone needs Your help. Show me the way through.

THINK ABOUT IT

Why does it seem easy to give in to temptation?
How does God help you to resist temptation?

BEYOND YOUR CONTROL

*[Jesus said], "Come to me, all you who are weary
and burdened, and I will give you rest. Take my yoke
upon you and learn from me, for I am gentle and
humble in heart, and you will find rest for your souls.
For my yoke is easy and my burden is light."*
MATTHEW 11:28–30

Father, when I'm tired and the weight of my life experience reaches a point of personal crisis, help me remember that You're in the business of crisis resolution. I will always face conflict, but You can give me rest even when everything seems out of control. You want to take my heavy burden, and it all starts when I come to You with only my weariness. You will exchange it for something so much better. Don't let me give up. Help me check in with You.

THINK ABOUT IT

*Why might it be hard to seek Jesus when you
struggle? Why would seeking Jesus seem to be
a choice that puts you at a disadvantage?*

CHOOSE LOVE

[Jesus said], A new commandment I give unto you,
That ye love one another; as I have loved you, that ye
also love one another. By this shall all men know that
ye are my disciples, if ye have love one to another.
JOHN 13:34–35 KJV

Dear God, if Christianity is a building, then love is Your most valuable building material. If Christianity were a porch, love would be the porch light. If Christianity were a celebration, love would be the invitation. Christianity is the result of Your love for me. My love for You and the people You created comes because You loved me first. I will never resemble You more than when I show love to others the way You have shown love to me. To love others is Your greatest command. Help me follow this command faithfully.

THINK ABOUT IT

Why do you think loving others is God's greatest
command? For you to love others more effectively,
why would Jesus need to love you first?

SPECK INSPECTIONS

*[Jesus said], "Why do you see the speck
that is in your brother's eye, but do not
notice the log that is in your own eye?"*
LUKE 6:41 ESV

Lord, it's way too easy to focus on the faults of others. I can wish they had a better relationship with You, to compare my successes with their failures, and wonder why people don't follow You better. I can remember they are human, and like me, they sin. If they are imperfect, then so am I. If they fail, so do I. If they need forgiveness, so do I. Accepting others doesn't mean I could ever forgive sin—that's Your doing. May I be honest enough to see that my own life is as much in need of help as anyone I ever meet. Then help me follow You more closely.

THINK ABOUT IT

*Why do you think people look down on
others? Why do people compare themselves
to others? What are some ways you can relate
to others that would answer this verse?*

LOVE SPEAKS TRUTH

We will not be influenced when people try to trick us with lies so clever they sound like the truth. Instead, we will speak the truth in love, growing in every way more and more like Christ, who is the head of his body, the church.
EPHESIANS 4:14–15 NLT

Father, sometimes the way people speak confuses me. They say something and it sounds like truth, but it's not. Sometimes they don't want to speak the truth. Sometimes they think a lie is more acceptable than the truth. But Your Word says I am to speak truth, and to show love. You say this helps me be more like You. If I don't speak the truth, I lie. If I don't love others, I either hate others, or I am indifferent to them. Help me always to combine love for people with the truth I learn from You.

THINK ABOUT IT

What negative result could occur if you spoke the truth, but didn't show love? What negative result could occur if you showed love, but didn't speak truth? Why do you need both?

GRATEFUL

*Enter his gates with thanksgiving, and his courts
with praise! Give thanks to him; bless his name!
For the LORD is good; his steadfast love endures
forever, and his faithfulness to all generations.*

PSALM 100:4–5 ESV

Lord, You invite me to talk to You at any time. When I'm in school, in the car, or with friends, I can pray. When I'm up in the middle of the night, You're still there to hear my concerns. When I start my conversations with You, may I be grateful, and may my words show You honor. You are faithful, and You always have been. You love me, and You've never stopped. You are good, and I can always count on Your goodness. Help me come to You with a heart that refuses to take You for granted.

THINK ABOUT IT

*Do you usually show gratitude to God when you
pray? Why or why not? Does gratitude to God
come naturally? Why or why not? How can You
show honor to God as part of your prayer life?*

THE PURSUIT

Pursue righteousness and a godly life, along with faith, love, perseverance, and gentleness. Fight the good fight for the true faith. Hold tightly to the eternal life to which God has called you, which you have declared so well before many witnesses.
1 TIMOTHY 6:11–12 NLT

Lord, if I'm in a race, I want to run toward a life that honors you. I want to get close to You. I want the purpose of my life to link with faith, love, endurance, and kindness. If I am to fight, may it be a good fight. A fight defending true faith. May I keep Your love a close companion. This is my pursuit. This is my prayer. This is my passion. And when I get off track, lead me back to the place where I recognize Your love, where I see Your path, and where I may walk with You once more.

THINK ABOUT IT

Why do you think the idea of a spiritual race makes sense to some people? Can you see your walk with Christ as a pursuit or race? How so?

SHINE

*"No one lights a lamp and then puts it under a
basket. Instead, a lamp is placed on a stand,
where it gives light to everyone in the house.
In the same way, let your good deeds shine
out for all to see, so that everyone will
praise your heavenly Father."*
MATTHEW 5:15–16 NLT

Dear God, I wouldn't put an empty cup over a flashlight if I needed it to see. I wouldn't hide a bonfire in a canyon if it needed to be seen. I wouldn't put a spotlight in a barn if I needed to light a stage. Light is meant to help me see something specific. It shines on what's hidden and helps me see where I'm going. When I let the light of my Christian life shine, let it mean something to those around me. May it light up those things that draw people to You.

THINK ABOUT IT

*How well do you think you're letting Your
spiritual light shine? When you were first
introduced to Jesus, who helped you see His
light the most? What can you learn from them?*

NO COMPLAINTS

Do everything without complaining and arguing,
so that no one can criticize you. Live clean, innocent
lives as children of God, shining like bright lights
in a world full of crooked and perverse people.
PHILIPPIANS 2:14–15 NLT

Father, I know my attitude is important to You. It's easy to see others not doing their best and complain, and it's easy to argue when I'm asked to do something that seems hard or unfair. But when I argue and complain, I give permission to other people to argue with me or complain about me. The life I want to live, and the example I want to follow, will reflect the light of Your love. The Bible says I live in a world filled with "crooked and perverse people." I believe it. You say I should live a "clean and innocent" life. I want to. Help me live a life that is different from what I so often see around me.

THINK ABOUT IT

Why do you think God puts a ban on arguments
and complaints? Why do you think arguing
can lead others to complain about you?

ANGER MANAGEMENT

Get rid of all bitterness, rage and anger, brawling
and slander, along with every form of malice.
Be kind and compassionate to one another, forgiving
each other, just as in Christ God forgave you.
EPHESIANS 4:31–32

Lord, I am learning that You are different than me. I am learning that You loved me when there was no reason to even like me. I am learning that You are kind, compassionate, and forgiving. I can't imagine You filled with bitterness, rage, or anger. I can't imagine you as someone who gets into fights, hurts the reputation of others, or holds a grudge. If Your love sets aside the idea of getting even, then I should follow Your example. My sin separates me from You. Your love removes my anger because Your compassion will always be the antidote. Use Your kindness to reverse my rage. Help me forgive, as You forgave me.

THINK ABOUT IT

When you are angry, do you first think of forgiving, or do you think of getting even? Why? How would things be different for you if God made decisions based on rage?

YOU CAN'T HIDE

O LORD, you have searched me and known me!
You know when I sit down and when I rise up; you
discern my thoughts from afar. You search out my
path and my lying down and are acquainted with
all my ways. Even before a word is on my tongue,
behold, O LORD, you know it altogether.
PSALM 139:1–4 ESV

Dear God, I can't hide anything from You. You know it all. I can't sit down, stand up, lie down, or walk alone without Your knowing. When it seems like I have no privacy, help me remember You stand guard, ready to help at a moment's notice because You know I will need help. When it comes to the words I speak, You know what I will say before I say it. That means You're waiting to help. Help me to ask for help sooner.

THINK ABOUT IT

Why should you be comfortable thinking that God
knows so much about you? Why would remembering
that God knows all about You leave you unsettled?

HONESTY

Search me, God, and know my heart; test me and know
my anxious thoughts. See if there is any offensive
way in me, and lead me in the way everlasting.
PSALM 139:23–24

Lord, if I'm honest, I admit that I am nervous praying about the ideas in these verses. It seems like an open invitation to seeing all the impure thoughts, anger, and rudeness that could easily describe me. And if You were to test me, I would fail. Because I've offended You. I know it. You know it. I struggle to admit it. But when I welcome You to see all I've done wrong, I also welcome Your offer to forgive. I welcome Your offer to lead me to a better way. Thank You for offering friendship after failure.

THINK ABOUT IT

How can inviting God to give You a spiritual exam
actually lead to a closer relationship with Him?
Why is it so hard to admit weakness? Why do you
think God wants you to be honest with Him?

THE LAWBREAKER

"If you ignore the least commandment and teach others to do the same, you will be called the least in the Kingdom of Heaven. But anyone who obeys God's laws and teaches them will be called great in the Kingdom of Heaven."
MATTHEW 5:19 NLT

Dear God, if I set aside, ignore, or even relax the importance of Your rules, I'm in the wrong. If I teach others to do the same, I'm in the wrong, If I pick and choose which rules to obey or not to obey, I'm in the wrong. Help me to remember that You didn't make rules to make life hard. Your rules aren't designed to allow one person to think they're better than another. Obeying your rules won't lead to being superior. Your rules are designed to protect, to inspire, and to bring me to a closeness I have always needed. Help me to remember that Your rules are important, but You are even more important.

THINK ABOUT IT

Why do you think someone might decide to ignore one of God's rules? Why do you think God's rules are important to follow?

THE WISDOM REQUEST

If any of you lacks wisdom, you should ask God, who gives generously to all without finding fault, and it will be given to you. But when you ask, you must believe and not doubt, because the one who doubts is like a wave of the sea, blown and tossed by the wind.

JAMES 1:5–6

Lord, when I need wisdom, You never say, "What's wrong? Can't you figure things out on your own?" You never find fault with the reasons behind my need to understand. I need to be comfortable in asking You for guidance, and I need to believe that You will share Your wisdom. I don't want my life to be like a ship without a rudder or a car without a steering wheel. You give direction in my journey and motivation in each adventure. Thank You for being generous, and for helping me see each step more clearly.

THINK ABOUT IT

How can wisdom give you better direction for your life? Why do you think it's easy to refuse to ask for God's directions?

THE PROBLEM WITH OPINIONS

Fools have no interest in understanding;
they only want to air their own opinions.
PROVERBS 18:2 NLT

Father, You want to give me wisdom, but when I try to discover wisdom without You, I'm acting foolishly. When I don't seek Your wisdom, all I have are opinions. I'm always willing to share, but what I share may not look very much like real wisdom. I act foolishly because whatever opinion I come up with never contains everything I would need to know to fully understand what You already know. My opinions lead to imperfect solutions, incorrect thinking, and wrong conclusions. Give me an interest in understanding. Help me talk more about Your truth than give my opinions. May Your wisdom change my thinking. May my thinking make Your wisdom the highest priority. And when I'm most interested in telling people what I think, remind me that You know more than me.

THINK ABOUT IT

Why is giving your opinion less helpful than
learning God's wisdom? Why do you think
it's foolish to refuse to learn from God?

USE YOUR WORDS

Don't use foul or abusive language. Let everything you say be good and helpful, so that your words will be an encouragement to those who hear them.
EPHESIANS 4:29 NLT

Dear God, I know the words I speak are important to You. My words can hurt others, damage reputations, and spread bitterness. On the other hand, they can also encourage, provide healing, and share truth. You want me to use my words to share good and helpful things. I don't want to speak words that abuse and offend. When the words I say don't match who I serve, help me to change what I say. Help me never to become a guy who is happy to see bad things happen to people. I want my mouth to represent You and share the encouragement You've shared with me.

THINK ABOUT IT

Have you ever considered how the words you use matter to God? How can you make your words good and helpful?

43

MORE THAN. . .

Do not love the world or the things in the world.
If anyone loves the world, the love of the Father is
not in him. For all that is in the world—the desires
of the flesh and the desires of the eyes and pride of
life—is not from the Father but is from the world.
1 John 2:15–16 esv

Lord, You tell me to love You and love people, but You don't want me to love things in the here and now so much that my love for You fades. Loving You in the here and now sounds like a great idea, but it's hard to do. I need to love You more than video games, cars, and girls. I need to love You more than cell phones, computers, and sports. I can appreciate what You've created, but I need to recognize that You will always be more important. Not sometimes. Always.

THINK ABOUT IT

Why do you think things can become more
important to you than God? What are
some of the benefits of loving God most?

EVERYTHING OR NOTHING

Without faith it is impossible to please him, for whoever
would draw near to God must believe that he exists
and that he rewards those who seek him.
HEBREWS 11:6 ESV

Dear God, if I want to please You, I have to believe You are real, not just a figment of my imagination. I need to trust that You have rewards when I make finding You my greatest quest. It's not enough to simply agree that there must be a God. I need to be convinced that You are worth trusting. That You are worth seeking. That You are worth more than anything I could possibly pursue. If I don't believe in You, I can't get close to You. If I don't believe in You, I can't expect answers to tough questions. You either mean everything to me, or You mean nothing. I need You to mean everything.

THINK ABOUT IT

Why is it impossible to pursue God with half
a heart? Why do you think it's important to
believe God is more than a good idea?

NOT ASHAMED

*I am not ashamed of this Good News about Christ. It is
the power of God at work, saving everyone who believes.*
ROMANS 1:16 NLT

Lord, I know that no one should be ashamed of the
Good News that You save people from sin. But there
are times when I've been more concerned with what
people will think if I talk about You than what You
will think if I don't. Help me never to be ashamed to
share Your story. When people hear about You, there
is power in the message. Knowing about Your love
for humanity leads people to know the power of rescue. They can't consider what You can do for them
unless they hear Your Good News. Let me be willing
to share what I know so that others may understand
they are welcome in Your family.

THINK ABOUT IT

*Why do we so often care more about what people
think than what God thinks? What can you do to
strengthen your conviction that God's Good News is
so important that you will share it with others?*

THE COMPASSIONATE ONE

For it is by grace you have been saved, through faith—
and this is not from yourselves, it is the gift of God—
not by works, so that no one can boast.
EPHESIANS 2:8–9

Dear God, if I could do something to pay for my own sin, I wouldn't need You. I could brag about the fact that I saved myself. But I can't pay for my own sins, and I can't brag. The only thing I can do is accept Your gift of rescue. It's hard to think there is nothing I could ever do to save myself, that nothing I could ever do that would impress You. The truth is, rescue is possible because You loved me. You will rescue other people as you rescued me, because You love them. Your rescue has nothing to do with whether I deserve it, and everything to do with Your compassion.

THINK ABOUT IT

Why do you think someone might try to earn
their own salvation? Why won't that work?

LOVE

Jesus replied, "'You must love the Lord your God
with all your heart, all your soul, and all your mind.'
This is the first and greatest commandment. A second
is equally important: 'Love your neighbor as yourself.'
The entire law and all the demands of the prophets
are based on these two commandments."
MATTHEW 22:37–40 NLT

Lord, Your Son, Jesus, said there were two great commandments. He said I should love You more than anyone or anything. But He also said I should love everyone else. Even when I don't agree with others, I should love them. Even when they annoy me, I should love them. Even when they seem like an enemy, I should love them. Every law You ever gave was linked to love. So help me use my heart, soul, and mind to love You, and to share what I learn about love with all people. The people You created.

THINK ABOUT IT

Why do you think love is so important to God?
Who showed love first? Why is that important?

MORE

We are human, but we don't wage war as humans do.
We use God's mighty weapons, not worldly weapons, to
knock down the strongholds of human reasoning and to
destroy false arguments. We destroy every proud obstacle
that keeps people from knowing God. We capture their
rebellious thoughts and teach them to obey Christ.
2 CORINTHIANS 10:3–5 NLT

Father, You want me to believe with the core of my being, and to think clearly with my mind. I can be kind in defending my faith in You. My words can be used by You to expose the arguments of others that don't sound like Your truth. I don't do this alone, and I don't do this to make myself look better than others. I need to have answers because people will have questions. I will need to know You more so I can share You more. Teach me—more.

THINK ABOUT IT

Why do you think keeping quiet about God is an
obstacle that keeps people from knowing Him? Why
do you think God wants to change people's thinking?

NEW-LIFE LIVING

*See what great love the Father has lavished on us,
that we should be called children of God! And that
is what we are! The reason the world does not know
us is that it did not know him. Dear friends, now we are
children of God, and what we will be has not yet been
made known. But we know that when Christ appears,
we shall be like him, for we shall see him as he is.*

1 JOHN 3:1–2

Dear God, Your love made me a member of Your family. If I'm misunderstood, it's because You're misunderstood. The more I make choices like You, the more peculiar I may seem to others. That difference can actually be attractive to people who are tired of thinking everyone must be the same. One day, when I get to see You face-to-face, I want my life to be more like Yours than mine.

THINK ABOUT IT

*Why should following God change the way
you act and react? How does it make you
feel to know that you are a child of God?*

A NEW NATURE

Put to death the sinful, earthly things lurking within you. . . . Now is the time to get rid of anger, rage, malicious behavior, slander, and dirty language.
COLOSSIANS 3:5, 8 NLT

Lord, when I came to know You, I received Your promise of new life, new nature, and new thinking. My life was filled with anger, bad behavior, speaking badly about others, and language that did not please You. Let me wear my new life in You like a favorite jacket, so others can see, recognize, and acknowledge that You're changing me. Help me make following You more important than following the urge to break Your rules. You want me to give sin a funeral. Following You must be incredibly important, because each new step either leads me toward or away from You.

THINK ABOUT IT

What is it about the idea of putting your old life to death that helps you see how important following God really is? How can you "wear" your new life?

GOD'S WILL

God's will is for you to be holy, so stay away from all sexual sin. Then each of you will control his own body and live in holiness and honor—not in lustful passion like the pagans who do not know God and his ways.
1 THESSALONIANS 4:3–5 NLT

Dear God, help me remember that my body is to be holy, set apart, and available to do what You want me to do. People who don't know You do things You don't want for me. By staying away from sexual sin, I'm showing You I understand that Your plan for that part of my life is more important, and that my actions today agree with Your plan. I can't reject what You say is Your will for my life.

THINK ABOUT IT

What does it mean to you to be holy and honorable in your relationship with God? Why is obedience to God's will so important?

ALWAYS A TIME TO SEEK

"Seek first the kingdom of God and his righteousness, and all these things will be added to you. Therefore do not be anxious about tomorrow, for tomorrow will be anxious for itself. Sufficient for the day is its own trouble."
MATTHEW 6:33–34 ESV

Father, when I'm anxious and feel like life is not going my way, when I think the things I need will never show up, and when I'm depressed and can't seem to find answers, help me remember that Your answer is to always seek You first. You shouldn't be an afterthought or a last hope. When I seek You above all, I don't have to be anxious about what may or may not happen to me. There is something very comforting about knowing that You can control what my anxiety can't. You have a plan, so help me seek You and stop worrying.

THINK ABOUT IT

Why do you think seeking God's righteousness takes away worries? How can you seek God first today?

START AND FINISH

*He who began a good work in you will carry it
on to completion until the day of Christ Jesus.*
PHILIPPIANS 1:6

Dear God, You never start something You have no intention of finishing. You created the world I now enjoy. You knew I needed to be rescued from my choice to sin, and I accepted rescue. You have introduced me to new-life living, and every day You give me the opportunity to learn more. When I obey what You ask of me, I am not only transformed, but I become more like the good work You began when I first believed. You must be very patient. I'm not always teachable. I can be rebellious. I make mistakes. But I want to become more like You every day, so keep working to make me into the man You need me to be.

THINK ABOUT IT

*How does it make you feel to know that
God doesn't give up on you? Why do you
think it's important that God is patient?*

THINK CLEARLY—WATCH CAREFULLY

Be alert and of sober mind. Your enemy the devil prowls around like a roaring lion looking for someone to devour. Resist him, standing firm in the faith, because you know that the family of believers throughout the world is undergoing the same kind of sufferings.

1 PETER 5:8–9

Lord, help me think clearly and watch carefully. I can't assume I'll never be attacked by the devil, but I can know that You will be with me. I'm not asked to attack the devil, but to resist him. I don't have to give in to temptation. I can stand my ground, trusting that You can help me say "No." When things are difficult, help me remember I've never been alone. There are Christians throughout the world who have Your help. You never failed them.

THINK ABOUT IT

What do you usually do when you're tempted to do something that breaks God's rules? Why is it important to remember that others face the same struggles?

TAKING CREDIT

Look here, you who say, "Today or tomorrow we are going to a certain town and will stay there a year. We will do business there and make a profit." How do you know what your life will be like tomorrow? Your life is like the morning fog—it's here a little while, then it's gone. What you ought to say is, "If the Lord wants us to, we will live and do this or that." Otherwise you are boasting about your own pretentious plans, and all such boasting is evil.

JAMES 4:13–16 NLT

Father, sometimes I believe that hard work is enough to be successful at what I do. Goals let me dream big. But I need to include You. If I don't admit that You can change my plans if You want to, then I am boasting that the plan was all mine. I am letting people think they don't need You when they make their plans. You call that evil.

THINK ABOUT IT

Why should you invite God to help with your plans? Why does God deserve credit for every good plan?

HELLO GOODBYE

My old self has been crucified with Christ. It is no longer I who live, but Christ lives in me. So I live in this earthly body by trusting in the Son of God, who loved me and gave himself for me.

GALATIANS 2:20 NLT

Lord, when I adjust to new-life living, I need to say goodbye to the life I used to live. My choices are no longer tied to a lack of wisdom. I have Your input, wisdom, and help. New-life living came at a price, but You paid it. You loved me, and Jesus gave Himself for me. I want to stop doing things that kept me away from You and start doing things that please You. My real life began the moment I said goodbye to my old self and said hello to You.

THINK ABOUT IT

Why is it important to say goodbye to the life you used to live? Why is it important to recognize that following Jesus means accepting a new way of living?

OVERWHELMING

If your enemy is hungry, feed him; if he is thirsty,
give him something to drink; for by so doing you
will heap burning coals on his head. Do not be
overcome by evil, but overcome evil with good.
ROMANS 12:20–21 ESV

Dear God, when someone is rude to me, I wonder if
I can repay them by being rude back, but that's not
what You want. I can give them food if they're hungry, and a bottle of water if they're thirsty. I don't
have to view them as an enemy, but simply as someone who needs to know You. It helps to remember
that being rude seems normal to those who don't
know You. There will always be evil in this world. I
don't want to be overwhelmed by the sins of others,
but I should want to overwhelm them with the incredible goodness that comes from You.

THINK ABOUT IT

Think about the ways God does things differently
than you do. How is His way better? How can you
overwhelm someone with God's goodness today?

WORDS

The tongue has the power of life and death,
and those who love it will eat its fruit.

PROVERBS 18:21

Lord, words are powerful. They can wound. They can heal. Words can give hope or cause people to believe a lie about themselves or others. What I say can speak life or cause the death of a dream. When I speak wounding words, I do not represent You well, and I make it harder for those who hear what I say to believe that You really do inspire new-life living. When I speak words of life, they welcome friendship and trust. I damage my reputation as a Christian when I freely say things that are unkind, untrue, and unloving. If words are an investment, help me choose words of life. May my words inspire others and sound like words that You would say.

THINK ABOUT IT

In what ways are wounding words easier to speak
than kind words? Why do you think it's important
to God that wounding words remain unspoken?

SOUNDS LIKE A FRIEND

A gentle answer deflects anger,
but harsh words make tempers flare.
PROVERBS 15:1 NLT

Dear God, the way I speak can make people defensive. I can speak critically and make an enemy. I can speak kindly and turn an enemy into someone who might hear me out. It's easy for me to shut down when people show hostility when they talk to me. I'm much more interested in knowing what others have to say when they treat me with respect. There are so many angry voices today that I choose to pay attention to those who speak with kindness. Help me be someone who uses kindness, compassion, and a gentle answer to bridge differences, someone who invites friendship. It's no wonder people avoid those who speak with harsh words. I don't ever want to stop speaking truth, but I want to share it as a friend and not an enemy.

THINK ABOUT IT

How can the way you speak differ from the way you
want to be spoken to? How can it be the same?

FROM THE BEGINNING

In the beginning the Word already existed. The Word was with God, and the Word was God. He existed in the beginning with God. God created everything through him, and nothing was created except through him.

JOHN 1:1–3 NLT

Father, Your Son, Jesus, is the Word made flesh. When the earth was created, He existed. When I think of You, I also think of Him. You created everything that exists through Your Son, and there is nothing in creation that He did not provide. Jesus wasn't an afterthought. He wasn't something that came along when God decided to rescue mankind. Jesus existed when the first waterfall took to gravity, when the first flower bloomed, when mankind spoke the first word. Jesus has been a part of Your story from the very beginning.

THINK ABOUT IT

Why do you think it's important that Jesus existed from the beginning? Why is it important that Jesus is God? Does this make Jesus more important than You thought? Why or why not?

ENTHUSIASTIC—UNMOVING

My dear brothers and sisters, be strong and immovable.
Always work enthusiastically for the Lord, for you know
that nothing you do for the Lord is ever useless.
1 CORINTHIANS 15:58 NLT

Lord, I need to be braver than I am, more courageous than I've ever been, and more unmoving than I am often inclined to be. Why? Your work, Your will, and Your way lead me to work in unwelcoming conditions, among ungrateful people saying ungodly things. May I be enthusiastic when few would blame me if I gave up, shut up, and sat down. You have given me a promise, and that promise is for all who follow You. There is nothing I can do for You that could ever be useless. From the smallest request for obedience to moments of personal sacrifice, may my answer to Your request to follow always be "Yes."

THINK ABOUT IT

Why is it easier to give up than stand up? Why do
you think the things done for God are important to
Him. Why should they be important to You?

ASSURED, AWARE, AND AVAILABLE

Rejoice in hope, be patient in
tribulation, be constant in prayer.
ROMANS 12:12 ESV

Dear God, Your hope assures me that You will do all
that You've promised. And I rejoice. The difficulties
I face are unpleasant. Teach me patience. I don't want
to face hard times alone. When I face hard times,
I will pray. When Jesus came to live on earth, He
was certain you loved Him. And He rejoiced. He
faced trouble, and he patiently endured. He took all
the time He needed to pray because it was You He
wanted to please most. I want my decisions to follow
His example. Help me remember that the best thing
I will ever do in my life is make myself available to
be transformed by Your love, grace, and mercy. May
my obedience make me assured of Your love, aware
that trouble is never forever, and that prayer is all
about a friendship with You.

THINK ABOUT IT

Does the command to rejoice seem like an
odd command? Why or why not? How does
prayer lead to a greater connection with God?

KNOW MORE

Be on your guard so that you may not be carried away by the error of the lawless and fall from your secure position. But grow in the grace and knowledge of our Lord and Savior Jesus Christ.
2 PETER 3:17–18

Father, it doesn't take long for me to hear opinions that don't sound like Your truth. It's easy for me to agree with error, or at least never correct error, though I know Your truth. I don't know if it's because I don't want people to think I'm weird, or maybe I struggle with the thought that they might make fun of me. I learned letters and numbers in kindergarten, but I needed to know more than that when I started school this year. Just as my knowledge improves in school, I want to grow up knowing You. Maybe next year I'll know even more.

THINK ABOUT IT

How can paying attention to the opinions of others hurt your relationship with God? How can you know more about God today?

WEAKNESS UNDERSTOOD

Since we have a great High Priest who has entered heaven, Jesus the Son of God, let us hold firmly to what we believe. This High Priest of ours understands our weaknesses, for he faced all of the same testings we do, yet he did not sin. So let us come boldly to the throne of our gracious God. There we will receive his mercy, and we will find grace to help us when we need it most.
HEBREWS 4:14–16 NLT

Heavenly Father, Jesus left earth and returned to You. His message was different than any other message mankind has ever heard. It's worth believing, sharing, and taking seriously. Your Son lived the life of a human. He faced temptation and stood strong every single time. I come to You as someone who understands human beings. Because You understand me, You offer mercy, grace, and help when I need it most.

THINK ABOUT IT

How does it make you feel knowing that Jesus faced the temptation to sin just as you do? Why does Jesus' experience make it easier to get close to God?

CALLED

I urge you to live a life worthy of the calling you have received. Be completely humble and gentle; be patient, bearing with one another in love. Make every effort to keep the unity of the Spirit through the bond of peace.
EPHESIANS 4:1–3

Dear God, You called me to be Your child. Your calling wasn't a suggestion, good idea, or vague invitation. You called, and I answered. Now You ask me to live the life of someone who's part of Your family. That life includes honoring You, putting others first, refusing to be rude, being willing to wait, and loving others even when they are being difficult. I want to be someone who promotes peace, welcomes unity, and learns from Your Spirit. Being part of Your family is a big deal. My purpose in life is following You.

THINK ABOUT IT

What does it mean to you to know that God called you to be part of His family? How should being a child of God change the way you respond to others?

ONE TEAM

There is one body and one Spirit—just as you were
called to the one hope that belongs to your call—
one Lord, one faith, one baptism, one God and Father
of all, who is over all and through all and in all.
EPHESIANS 4:4–6 ESV

Father, You have one team led by one coach. You have one goal, and You promise Your team that they win even when the game is especially hard. You have one team captain and one belief in Your game plan. There is one team spirit with one team owner. I know that's not exactly what the verses say, but it helps me understand that Your family has to work together just like any other team. I can't win alone, or join another team, or badmouth my teammates or my coach. Help me be a team player and let You lead.

THINK ABOUT IT

How is it helpful to remember you are part
of God's team? How does it help to know
that it is God who leads the team?

WAITING TO BE FOUND

The LORD says, "I was ready to respond, but no one
asked for help. I was ready to be found, but no one
was looking for me. I said, 'Here I am, here I am!'
to a nation that did not call on my name."

ISAIAH 65:1 NLT

Dear God, once I needed help, and You offered help.
But I didn't accept Your help. Once You were ready to
be found, but I thought I was looking for something
else. It was clear You were ready and waiting for me.
But I ignored You. There are lots of people like me.
But You aren't hiding. You don't make it hard to find
You. You've made an offer to help and, like me, there
are many who think Your offer is too good to be true.
But it is true. It is good. Thanks for the help.

THINK ABOUT IT

What does it mean to you to know that God
wants to be found? How does it help for you to
know that God wants you to ask Him for help?

ACCEPT HELP

*Live wisely among those who are not believers,
and make the most of every opportunity. Let your
conversation be gracious and attractive so that
you will have the right response for everyone.*
COLOSSIANS 4:5–6 NLT

Dear God, I'm convinced I can't live the life You want me to live if You don't help me. I can't live the life You want me to live if I don't accept Your help. Help me take opportunities to tell people about You. May the words I speak, and the way I say those words, be filled with grace, so people will trust what I say. May my conversation be acceptable to You and understandable to others. Help me know more so I can share more, I can love more, I can reach more, I can follow more, and I can learn more.

THINK ABOUT IT

*Why do you think it's important to God that
the way you speak about Him is something
worth listening to? What will you need to
do to share the right response with others?*

IT WAS YOU

*Consider your calling, brothers: not many of you were
wise according to worldly standards, not many were
powerful, not many were of noble birth. But God chose
what is foolish in the world to shame the wise; God
chose what is weak in the world to shame the strong.*

1 CORINTHIANS 1:26–27 ESV

Father, You give responsibility to people who have
never been the valedictorian of their class. You
have a purpose for people who have never been a
senator. You have a plan for people who have never
been a prince. That's most people. You take normal
people who seem common and unworthy and give
them wisdom they can't learn in school and strength
they can't develop in a gym. And even those who
are among the smartest and strongest can't figure
out how that growth happened. It was You, God. It
was You.

THINK ABOUT IT

*Why do you think God uses people who society
thinks are foolish and weak to do big things?
How does His plan encourage you?*

POWERFUL AND EFFECTIVE

*The prayer of a righteous person
is powerful and effective.*
JAMES 5:16

God, when I pray to You, there are times it seems like I'm not really talking to anyone. I say words, but I'm not sure they're getting through, and sometimes they even feel like I'm just saying things I've memorized but don't really mean. I want my conversation with You to be something I look forward to. I don't want to feel like I pray because I'm just supposed to. Because prayer is a conversation, help me take the time to listen as much as I talk. I believe prayer can change me, and I want to be changed. I believe prayer can bring me closer to You, and I want to be close. I believe prayer means something to You, and I want to please You. May you make our conversations powerful and effective.

THINK ABOUT IT

*How can an improved prayer life lead
to a greater connection with God? When
can you start an improved prayer life?*

A BETTER CHOICE

The sinful nature wants to do evil, which is just the opposite of what the Spirit wants. And the Spirit gives us desires that are the opposite of what the sinful nature desires. These two forces are constantly fighting each other, so you are not free to carry out your good intentions.
GALATIANS 5:17 NLT

Lord, sometimes I forget that what You want me to do will always be better for me than what I want to do. And if I disagree with Your plan, help me remember Yours is always the right plan. It's amazing to me how often what I want to do is the opposite of what You want me to do. Two different ideas—two perspectives—one choice to make. When my choice to sin conflicts with Your command to do the right thing help me make Your choice. I want my good intentions to be great decisions.

THINK ABOUT IT

Why do you think you struggle with wanting your way over God's way? Why is it never enough to have good intentions?

SPIRITUAL NAVIGATION

*Let the Holy Spirit guide your lives. Then you
won't be doing what your sinful nature craves.*
GALATIANS 5:16 NLT

Father, You have one incredible spiritual navigation
system. You know each destination and how long it
should take for me to get from where I am to where
I'm supposed to be. When I pay attention to Your
leadership, I stay on track. When I don't pay attention to Your navigation, I don't arrive on time and
have less interest in where You're taking me. The
sinful nature I was born with always struggles to get
its way. When I pay attention to You, I'm paying less
attention to the things which cause me to choose sin.
I don't do well with two sets of directions. Your plan
and my sin will not lead me to the same destination.
Help me follow Your navigation.

THINK ABOUT IT

*Why will there always be a struggle when you
know God's plan but choose your own way?
Why will your way often lead to a choice to sin?*

THE WANT TO

*As obedient children, do not conform to the evil desires
you had when you lived in ignorance. But just as he
who called you is holy, so be holy in all you do.*
1 PETER 1:14–15

Dear God, when I was younger, there was someone I
wanted to be like. I wanted to do everything just like
they did. When they warned me about something,
I avoided it. When they told me it was good to do
something, I did it. When I saw them do something,
I wanted to do it too. Sometimes there were other
voices, and they didn't always agree with the one I
wanted to listen to. But You want me to be like You.
You have always wanted me to follow where You lead
me, learn what You teach me, and share what You
give me. I can follow in Your footsteps—I just need
to want to.

THINK ABOUT IT

*Why do you think Jesus' example is worth
following? How does following Jesus equal
obedience? How can you be more like Him?*

OBEDIENT TRUST

We can be sure that we know him if we obey his
commandments. If someone claims, "I know God,"
but doesn't obey God's commandments, that person
is a liar and is not living in the truth. But those who
obey God's word truly show how completely they
love him. That is how we know we are living in him.
1 JOHN 2:3–5 NLT

Father, I wouldn't be expected to obey You if I didn't know You. But since I do, there is every reason to expect that I honor You by obeying Your rules. It's hard to believe that someone knows You when they don't even want to obey. Your Word calls them a liar, someone who doesn't accept Your truth. I can show how much I love You by knowing, accepting, and following Your rules.

THINK ABOUT IT

If it is important to obey God when You know
who He is, why is it so hard to obey Him?
Why is there a struggle to expect people
who don't know God to obey Him?

HONOR

*Give honor to marriage, and remain faithful to one
another in marriage. God will surely judge people
who are immoral and those who commit adultery.*
HEBREWS 13:4 NLT

Dear God, help me see that the closest relationship
I can have on earth needs to be honored by waiting
until I get married. Then, if I get married, I want to
be faithful to my wife by keeping that close relationship only with her. You say that You judge those who
make the wrong choice before marriage or aren't
faithful after marriage. I am glad You offer forgiveness, but help me be wise enough to honor You in
how I deal with who I date and marry. It can be easy
to think of this time in life as just having fun, but You
say that this time is important to You, important for
me, and important to the development of honor.

THINK ABOUT IT

*Why is honor toward girls so important to
God? How can your choices in dating
impact faithfulness in marriage?*

WHAT'S A HEART?

Keep your heart with all vigilance,
for from it flow the springs of life.
PROVERBS 4:23 ESV

Lord, the thing You call my heart is what makes me who I am. It's not just my mind. It's something more. And I gave this part of my life to You when I accepted Your gift of rescue. You can change the decisions I make by changing my heart, which matters more than knowledge, emotion, or logic. My heart is the place where You speak to me and where my faith grows. But You also say my heart is wicked and unknowable. Maybe that's why giving my heart to You just makes sense. You know how to change something I can never truly understand into something You can use. Soften my hard heart and continue to do the work only You can do to make me new.

THINK ABOUT IT

How can the heart be a place where faith grows and
a place that entertains wickedness at the same time?
Why is your heart a great gift to give to God?

THE PURPOSE OF THE PATH

How can a young person stay on the path
of purity? By living according to your word.
PSALM 119:9

Father, if purity is a path, how do I recognize it, and
how do I stay on it? Sometimes I act like purity is
something unrealistic, or so far out of reach that I
don't even try, but You want me to try. You want me
to do what You've asked me to do. My journey in
purity lies in a relationship and not in a spiritual
checklist. If I live according to what You say in Your
Word, I should learn more about who You are and
what You want. Help me refuse to treat my relationship with You like a burden, doing things I don't
want to do. I want to see my relationship with You as
a way of learning a better way of living from the God
who shares words of life with an unworthy me.

THINK ABOUT IT

Is the path of purity really important?
Why or why not? What does it mean
to live according to God's Word?

HARVEST WHAT YOU PLANT

Don't be misled—you cannot mock the justice of God. You will always harvest what you plant. Those who live only to satisfy their own sinful nature will harvest decay and death from that sinful nature. But those who live to please the Spirit will harvest everlasting life from the Spirit.

GALATIANS 6:7–8 NLT

Lord, I can't ask You to do something You've never promised. I can't ask You to excuse my sin, give me whatever I ask for, or trust me to make perfect choices. To believe You would ever go against Your truth means I don't understand You very well. If I plant seeds of deception, I can't expect a truth tree to grow. The choices I make will grow a crop that either proves I'm following You or a crop that urges me to come to You for help.

THINK ABOUT IT

Is it possible to plant a corn seed and expect a flower to grow? Why or why not? How can this apply to the life of a Christ follower?

HIGH-SOUNDING NONSENSE

*Don't let anyone capture you with empty philosophies
and high-sounding nonsense that come from human
thinking and from the spiritual powers of this
world, rather than from Christ.*
COLOSSIANS 2:8 NLT

Dear God, I don't want to let anyone talk me out of following You. People will have creative ideas to explain the way things work. It can sound clever. It can sound convincing. But when those ideas contradict the ideas I find in the Bible, help me reject what Your Word rejects. Maybe it all comes down to who I trust more and whose voice I most want to hear. Help me send "high-sounding nonsense" to my inner DELETE file. And if I'm never to let anyone capture me with this nonsense, I really need to know what You have to say about the matter. Help me search. Help me study. Help me be steady in my trust in You.

THINK ABOUT IT

*Why do you think it is so easy to consider certain
ideas you've never considered before? Why do you
think the Bible warns against accepting these ideas?*

TRUTH VS. MYTH

*For the time is coming when people will not endure
sound teaching, but having itching ears they will
accumulate for themselves teachers to suit their
own passions, and will turn away from listening
to the truth and wander off into myths.*

2 TIMOTHY 4:3–4 ESV

Father, You're the owner of true words. Your words inspire real life. Your life is the only one worthy to follow. When I struggle with believing something, don't let me seek out people who disagree with You. I can always find people who will tell me what I want to hear. What I need is to interact with people who will encourage me to look for Your truth. I don't want to say that I'm following You and then reject Your wisdom. Your Word isn't open to creative interpretation. Give me wisdom to understand what I read, the courage to believe it, and the strength to follow it.

THINK ABOUT IT

*Why do some people pick and choose what they
want to believe from the Bible? Is the Bible
the only source for truth? Why or why not?*

MAKING STUFF UP

This is my prayer: that your love may abound more
and more in knowledge and depth of insight, so that
you may be able to discern what is best and may
be pure and blameless for the day of Christ.
PHILIPPIANS 1:9–10

Dear God, I want to know more about You and to understand what I'm learning. That will help me love You more. I want to be able to determine the difference between what someone believes and whether You agree with it. I don't want to be rude to that person, but I want You to help me avoid wrong thinking. Making up what I want to believe means I have decided You don't really know everything, and that I can't trust You. I want Your love to work in me so that it's easier to believe that what You say is what You mean.

THINK ABOUT IT

Why is it important to notice when someone is not
speaking the truth? How can knowing the difference
between truth and untruth improve Your decisions?

WISDOM CHASE

*My son, if you receive my words and treasure up my
commandments with you, making your ear attentive
to wisdom and inclining your heart to understanding;
yes, if you call out for insight and raise your voice for
understanding, if you seek it like silver and search for
it as for hidden treasures, then you will understand the
fear of the Lord and find the knowledge of God.*

PROVERBS 2:1–5 ESV

Father, truth is a pursuit. I want to race it and chase it
until it becomes a close companion. I need to accept
Your truth, to view it as a treasure, to keep my ear in
tune with Your wisdom, and to point my heart in the
direction of truth. Seeking Your thoughts is greater
than a treasure hunt, and I can call out for it. In the
end of my wisdom chase, I find You.

THINK ABOUT IT

*How does it change your perspective to think
that God wants you to pursue His wisdom?
Have you ever thought of seeking God's
wisdom as an adventure? Why or why not?*

UNHEALTHY ARROGANCE

*Some people may contradict our teaching, but these are
the wholesome teachings of the Lord Jesus Christ. These
teachings promote a godly life. Anyone who teaches
something different is arrogant and lacks understanding.
Such a person has an unhealthy desire to quibble over
the meaning of words. This stirs up arguments ending in
jealousy, division, slander, and evil suspicions. These
people always cause trouble. Their minds are corrupt,
and they have turned their backs on the truth. To them,
a show of godliness is just a way to become wealthy.*
1 Timothy 6:3–5 nlt

Lord, Your teachings promote a godly life. When
someone teaches something unwholesome, You
call them arrogant, unhealthy, and corrupt. At some
point I will encounter someone whose arguments
cause people to be divided, suspicious, to speak
badly about others, and to express evil in many different ways. Help me avoid their arguments by reading and believing Your Word.

THINK ABOUT IT

*What does the verse suggest is the source
of wholesome teachings? Who does the
verse suggest lacks understanding?*

SELECTIVE

*The LORD said unto Samuel, Look not on his
countenance, or on the height of his stature;
because I have refused him: for the LORD seeth
not as man seeth; for man looketh on the outward
appearance, but the LORD looketh on the heart.*
1 SAMUEL 16:7 KJV

Dear God, there are times when I'm certain I can tell
who's not eligible to become a Christian. I look at
their actions and think they would never have any
interest in knowing You. I can even see a look in
their eyes, or a hairstyle, or the friends they hang out
with, and I'm ready to give up on them. But when
the prophet Samuel was looking to name a new
king, and he thought he found him, You said that
You look at the heart and not what a man looks like.
Help me remember everyone is a possible brother or
sister in You.

THINK ABOUT IT

*Does God see things the same way you do?
Why or why not? If God sees things one way
and you see them another, who's right?*

THE VINE

[Jesus said] "Yes, I am the vine; you are the branches. Those who remain in me, and I in them, will produce much fruit. For apart from me you can do nothing."
JOHN 15:5 NLT

Lord, Your Son proclaimed that He was the vine. He promised to be the one to make sure His family of branches had all of the spiritual nutrition they would need. So if I try to separate myself from Your Son, I no longer have the ability to grow spiritual fruit. The truth is that I can do nothing meaningful on my own. You are not a take-it-or-leave-it God. I'm either all in or I'm not in at all. Following You isn't a part-time effort for those moments when I'm available. If real life comes from You, You are the vine. Keep me attached and help me bear much fruit for You.

THINK ABOUT IT

How does the word picture of a vine and branch help you understand your connection to Jesus? Why do you think you are incapable of doing meaningful things on your own?

GO

"Therefore go and make disciples of all nations, baptizing them in the name of the Father and of the Son and of the Holy Spirit, and teaching them to obey everything I have commanded you. And surely I am with you always, to the very end of the age."
MATTHEW 28:19–20

Dear God, sometimes I'm quiet at moments when I should be talking about You. In the military, officers receive orders providing the opportunity to lead other soldiers on a mission. You want me to be a leader in sharing Your best news. It is your Great Commission. I can't lead with my mouth closed and my feet unwilling to go where You send me. I'm supposed to help people learn, to show them what it looks like to obey You. And when I help people learn about You, You promise to go with me. Your news is worth sharing—everywhere.

THINK ABOUT IT

Why do you think God doesn't want you to keep His rescue plan secret? Did you know you were called to be a leader? How does that make you feel?

LIFELONG LEARNING

"Students are not greater than their teacher. But the student who is fully trained will become like the teacher."
Luke 6:40 NLT

Lord, why should I think You can't be known? If You are willing to teach, why should I be convinced I'm unteachable? If I'm a student, why do I seem to skip Your classes? I'm not greater than You, and I never will be. I'm a student, and if I make myself available to be fully trained, I will become more like You. You are my Teacher. Training may take the rest of my life, but as each day passes, this student understands You more and follows You with more heart, soul, mind, and strength. May I continue to attend Your classes, put what I learn to good use, and share what I'm learning so others may see the value in joining Your class.

THINK ABOUT IT

How does it help to think of learning from God as something a student would do? Why would a Christian want to be fully trained?

ENCOURAGE

*Let us consider how we may spur one another
on toward love and good deeds, not giving
up meeting together, as some are in the habit
of doing, but encouraging one another.*
HEBREWS 10:24–25

Father, You have never wanted me to be alone in my walk with You. I know You walk with me. But You also encourage me to walk with others who trust You with their lives and futures. And when I do walk with other members of Your family, help me think of ways that I can encourage them to keep walking, to stay faithful, and to stick with Your plan. When I think that staying away from Your family is a good choice, please help me remember that this is a habit too many are falling into. You say my Christian family is important, so keep me from taking a vacation from them. Help me really love them.

THINK ABOUT IT

*Why is it important to invest some of your time
in encouraging other Christians? Why is it
important to stay connected with other Christians?*

NO DISTRACTIONS

The LORD is my light and my salvation;
whom shall I fear? the LORD is the strength
of my life; of whom shall I be afraid?
PSALM 27:1 KJV

Dear God, You help me see where I need to go. You provide me with the strength my life needs. You offer rescue and keep me safe. You're there for me, so why should I let anything distract me from where You lead? Help me trust in Your rescue plan and the strength that can only come from You. There are all kinds of things that pull me away from You, and sometimes I am led away too quickly, too easily. A bad case of forgetfulness. You know the way, so help me stop looking for non-answers in unproven places through those who are not in You. Show Your strength, be my light, and chase my fear from its hiding place.

THINK ABOUT IT

If God is for you, why does fear try so hard to get
your attention? If God has a rescue plan, why does
it seem some people can make you doubt Him?

THE CHASE

Don't love money; be satisfied with what
you have. For God has said, "I will never
fail you. I will never abandon you."
HEBREWS 13:5 NLT

Dear God, sometimes I pay more attention to the things I have than to the gifts You offer. When I love money and all the things it can buy, I'm not looking far enough ahead. The things I can buy will break, get old, and become worthless. But You never fail. You never age. Your value never ceases to grow. I can be much more satisfied when I live with what I have as long as I have access to You. If my life in You is an investment, there is more to gain from walking with You than in buying things. There's more value in being satisfied than in chasing after things with an expiration date.

THINK ABOUT IT

Why is satisfaction more important than what
money can buy? Why is it more important to
remember that God never fails or abandons
than to think about your next purchase?

FEAR IS NO MATCH FOR PEACE

Do not be anxious about anything, but in every situation, by prayer and petition, with thanksgiving, present your requests to God. And the peace of God, which transcends all understanding, will guard your hearts and your minds in Christ Jesus.

PHILIPPIANS 4:6–7

Father, I want this prayer to send my anxiety away on a one-way trip. With this prayer, and in this request, may I bring my concerns to You. I want to share my gratitude, to believe Your promises, and to remember that there is no bad time to pray. I'm thankful that my fears are no match for Your peace. My prayers are matched by Your answers. And when I don't understand how it happened, help me remember that Your peace stands like a soldier protecting all that I think and believe. With You there is no reason to fear.

THINK ABOUT IT

Why should fear always trigger a need to pray? Why is it important that God protects your heart and mind in times of fear?

WORKING TOGETHER, AND GOOD

We know that all things work together for
good to them that love God, to them who
are the called according to his purpose.
ROMANS 8:28 KJV

Lord, bad things happen to good people. Bad things happen to bad people. Bad days are typical when you live in a society where many people don't follow You. But when it seems like circumstances try to ruin my life, help me remember that You have the power to take the worst things that can happen and put all the pieces together somehow—not only make it okay, but really good. I may not see how it happened today or even this year, but when I love You and follow Your purpose for my life, I can expect Your help, comfort, and love. You handle what I don't understand and prove You're more than capable of taking care of everything.

THINK ABOUT IT

Who can expect that God will work things together
for good? How many things can God take care of?

COMFORT

All praise to God, the Father of our Lord Jesus Christ.
God is our merciful Father and the source of all comfort.
He comforts us in all our troubles so that we can comfort
others. When they are troubled, we will be able to give
them the same comfort God has given us.

2 Corinthians 1:3–4 NLT

Dear God, life can be hard, and when it is, You offer comfort. Your comfort is a great mixture of peace, relief, and contentment. It leaves me satisfied, knowing that You're compassionate and capable. When I'm certain You have everything under control, I'm comforted, and I can comfort others. Because You've helped me see what that looks like. You thought it was important enough to show me firsthand how to comfort others, and You showed me that even when trouble comes, I should be there to provide comfort.

THINK ABOUT IT

Why is it important that Christians understand
the need for God's comfort and the need to
comfort others? What does that understanding
teach you about the trouble you face?

THE RACE

*Brothers and sisters, I do not consider myself yet
to have taken hold of it. But one thing I do: Forgetting
what is behind and straining toward what is ahead,
I press on toward the goal to win the prize for which
God has called me heavenward in Christ Jesus.*

PHILIPPIANS 3:13–14

Lord, I'm in a race, and I want to win it. But I haven't reached the finish line, so I don't want to act like I have. I'm in the race, but sometimes I act like I'm not. Help me admit my mistakes, but also to forget my past. Because You rescued me, You trained me, and You marked the course for my race. Help me be bold with each new step. Help me do everything I can to move toward Your goals. Allow me to grow until the day I meet You face-to-face in heaven.

THINK ABOUT IT

*In what ways does it help to think of
your walk with Jesus as a race? Why is
it important to forget what is behind you?*

TRADING THE OLD FOR THE NEW

*Don't lie to each other, for you have stripped off
your old sinful nature and all its wicked deeds.
Put on your new nature, and be renewed as you
learn to know your Creator and become like him.*

Colossians 3:9–10 nlt

Father, You said that every human would sin. You
said that I should admit that I have broken Your
rules. You say that I should not tell other people
things that aren't true. Help me give up the worn-out
clothes of my sinful past for the beautiful clothing
of new-life living. I need to learn that my old-nature
clothes are unattractive, and that I will always look
better when I look like You. Renew my interest in
Your Word, Your plan, and Your love. Help me want
to know You more. Help me disobey You less.

THINK ABOUT IT

*Why is it important to God that you don't
lie to others? How interested are you
in becoming more like God?*

WE ARE

*There is neither Jew nor Gentile, neither
slave nor free, nor is there male and female,
for you are all one in Christ Jesus.*
GALATIANS 3:28

Lord, You made sure from the beginning that Your Word was clear. You don't separate people the way everyone else does. You don't love the people of one nation more than another—You love them all. You don't think that people who have been oppressed are less worth loving than those who haven't. You don't make a choice between men and women. You love everyone. When I became a Christ follower, I became something more than my culture, my gender, or my employment status. The things that normally divide people are supposed to go away when You gain a new follower. We are all different, but we are different together. We are all loved. Forever.

THINK ABOUT IT

*Why is it important that God loves everyone?
What can you learn from the way God treats
His people? How can you put what you've
learned from God into action? Will you?*

THE WAY HE HELPS

*Take delight in the L*ord*, and he will give you*
your heart's desires. Commit everything you do
*to the L*ord*. Trust him, and he will help you.*
PSALM 37:4–5 NLT

Lord, You never said I should expect You to give me whatever I want. When Your Word says that You will give me the desires of my heart, it first says that I need to take delight in You. When I selfishly ask for things, I'm taking delight in what I want and not seeking to honor You with my request. When You offer help, You also ask me to make sure I let You manage my plans and trust You with the outcome. Help me be grateful for Your help, but also to remember that when I follow You, I learn to desire the things that already have Your approval.

THINK ABOUT IT

Why do you think it would be reckless for God to give
you anything you wanted? How can you take delight
in God, and commit everything You do to Him?

I FEEL ALONE

*Come quickly, L*ORD*, and answer me, for my depression*
deepens. Don't turn away from me, or I will die.
Let me hear of your unfailing love each morning,
for I am trusting you. Show me where to walk,
for I give myself to you.
PSALM 143:7–8 NLT

Father, when I wake up and it seems like everything
I encounter turns bad, I sometimes wonder if You're
as good as I thought. Depression seems my only
companion, and I feel that You're not near, and that
maybe You don't care. But I'm wrong. You do care.
You are there. But when I feel this way, I sense I'm
sinking and there's no life jacket in sight. Please
don't turn away when I feel stuck in a depression
swamp. Answer me. I will have questions. Show up.
Help me see where to place my next step. May my
trust in you outweigh my fear of feeling alone.

THINK ABOUT IT

When you feel depressed, what is your first response?
How do these verses suggest a better response?

ONE CAME TO TAKE

"The thief comes only to steal and kill and destroy.
I came that they may have life and have it abundantly."
JOHN 10:10 ESV

Dear God, the only one who wants to see me depressed and broken is Satan. He doesn't show up and speak words of comfort or offer encouragement. He doesn't show kindness. He has another motive. The adversary arrives on a mission to steal my hope and destroy my life. So when bad days come and I'm willing to listen to negative words, help me remember that abundant life is Your gift. Everyone wants hope. Everyone wants kindness and encouragement. When my enemy shows up, help me pull the welcome mat from the front door of my life. Put out NO TRESPASSING signs. Keep my heart's door locked. I don't want Satan ruining my life. But as much as I can prepare, it still doesn't do any good if You aren't here. Come soon. I need Your help.

THINK ABOUT IT

What does this verse suggest leads to daily
struggles? Who offers abundant life?

ONE CAME TO GIVE

*The faithful love of the LORD never ends! His mercies
never cease. Great is his faithfulness; his mercies
begin afresh each morning. I say to myself, "The LORD
is my inheritance; therefore, I will hope in him!"*
LAMENTATIONS 3:22–24 NLT

Lord, there may be days when my enemies leave me
alone, but You never do. If I am attacked, it will not
be forever, because I am loved by You. There will
never be an end to Your kindness, mercy, and hope.
When You make a promise, You never fail to keep it.
When I wake up, I can be sure You will keep me company. When I look around me and everything seems
to break, fail, or come to an end, I need to remember
that it's just not true of You. Help me remember that
You came to guide me through those days.

THINK ABOUT IT

*When does God's love end? When will His mercies
cease? When will He leave and forsake you?
Who offers a future that's unbreakable?*

WITH YOU

The LORD is good to those whose hope is in him,
to the one who seeks him; it is good to wait
quietly for the salvation of the LORD.
LAMENTATIONS 3:25–26

Father, I don't need to throw a fit when bad days come. I need to pray and wait for Your rescue. That doesn't mean I can't or shouldn't talk to anyone, it just means that Your answer is worth waiting for. My hope is not wishful thinking, but an assurance that the only one who can figure out my problem is You. I will seek You first. I will wait as long as I need to. There are many ways people deal with the days when their struggle is more real than they thought possible. Help me remember that You don't just help me cope, You handle every detail of my pain.

THINK ABOUT IT

Why do you think getting angry rarely makes
bad days better? How do you think seeking
God can change the outcome of a bad day?

THE FAITHFUL

We are not like those who turn away from God to
their own destruction. We are the faithful ones.
HEBREWS 10:39 NLT

Lord, don't let me cheer for my choices. Help me
cheer for the God who made the choices possible. I follow You because You are worth following.
The choice I made is a choice anyone can make. The
ones that choose You are the faithful ones. The ones
that walk away are on a path that leads to destruction. My help comes from You alone. I am rescued
from sin. If I can join with others and call myself
faithful it is only because You were faithful first. You
gave, and I accepted. You shared, and I discovered.
You arrived and suddenly I had a choice. I accepted,
and I can only be grateful. I can only pray that I will
be faithful.

THINK ABOUT IT

God is faithful to you, but why is it important
for you to be faithful to Him? Why is turning
away from God such a bad idea?

BETTER THINKING

Finally, all of you, have unity of mind, sympathy,
brotherly love, a tender heart, and a humble mind.
Do not repay evil for evil or reviling for reviling,
but on the contrary, bless, for to this you were called.
1 PETER 3:8–9 ESV

Dear God, I need to connect with Your faithful ones. Your family deserves my attention. May we work together. Help my life show compassion, love, gentleness, and thinking that doesn't demand first place. Getting even is not something You encourage. I read that You want me to bless others, and I read that this is part of my calling. It's much harder to show mercy than justice, but it is what You ask of Your family. It's what You ask of me.

THINK ABOUT IT

Why is it important to know how to live with
other people? What surprises you most in the
choices God asks you to make in relationships?

INTERESTED

Don't be selfish; don't try to impress others.
Be humble, thinking of others as better than
yourselves. Don't look out only for your own
interests, but take an interest in others, too. You
must have the same attitude that Christ Jesus had.
<small>PHILIPPIANS 2:3–5 NLT</small>

Lord, I want my own way. I want to feel important.
I think that's how most people feel. But You say I
should not demand my way or try to impress others.
You want me to see the good in other people even
when they are better at something than me. Your
Son, Jesus, came to this world and took an interest
in others. He was humble, and that's the attitude I
need. Teach me to stop pointing at myself when I
should be pointing to You. Your solutions, Your compassion, and Your interest in others is better than
mine. It always has been, and it always will be.

THINK ABOUT IT

Why do you think people try to impress others?
Why do you think God appreciates
humility more than selfishness?

BETTER FRIENDS

*Two are better than one, because they have a good
return for their labor: If either of them falls down,
one can help the other up. But pity anyone who
falls and has no one to help them up. Though one
may be overpowered, two can defend themselves.*
ECCLESIASTES 4:9–10

Dear God, friendship is important to You. You want
to be my friend, and You want me to prove to others that I have learned how to be a friend. If I were
to spend all my time alone, where would encouragement come from? If I said I didn't need help,
where would help come from? If I am overpowered
by emotion, who could I welcome into that personal
moment? Teach me to be friends with You first, and
then to seek out someone who has learned Your lessons in friendship.

THINK ABOUT IT

*Can you name three benefits you have discovered
about friendship? Why do you think friendship is
important to God? How can you take what you
learned today and become a better friend?*

UNITY PLAN

*Is there any encouragement from belonging to
Christ? Any comfort from his love? Any fellowship
together in the Spirit? Are your hearts tender and
compassionate? Then make me truly happy by agreeing
wholeheartedly with each other, loving one another,
and working together with one mind and purpose.*
PHILIPPIANS 2:1–2 NLT

Father, I will answer these questions. I'm encouraged because I belong to You. I'm comforted because You love me. I'm in good company when Your Spirit is there to teach me. When I'm with You, my heart grows large, and I am able to show Your compassion to others. Help me to better demonstrate Your love, unity, and purpose. Sometimes this life is hard. Sometimes I find it difficult to change my way of thinking to match Your instruction. Sometimes it just doesn't make sense. But when I follow, I begin to see the wisdom in Your plan of unity for Your family on earth.

THINK ABOUT IT

*What does the phrase, "working together with
one mind and purpose" mean to you? Why
is this important in the Christian life?*

LOVE'S TEST

If anyone has material possessions and sees a brother or sister in need but has no pity on them, how can the love of God be in that person? Dear children, let us not love with words or speech but with actions and in truth.
1 JOHN 3:17–18

Dear God, You've made it simple for me to tell if my actions show Your love. If I see someone in need, and I have a way to help but I don't, I'm not showing love. If Your love has taught me compassion but I don't show compassion, then I'm not showing love. Your Word even questions whether I have allowed Your love to change me. Let me never leave love up to emotions and empty promises. Help me put compassionate love high on my priority list. May the truth of my words show up in my actions.

THINK ABOUT IT

What are two ways you can share God's love? Why do you think love and action go together?

A DAILY PURSUIT

Don't let anyone think less of you because you are young.
Be an example to all believers in what you say, in the
way you live, in your love, your faith, and your purity.
1 TIMOTHY 4:12 NLT

Lord, I want to be thought as someone who has grown up. I don't want to be treated like a kid. I'm young, but I can be an example to people who are younger than me. I can even be an example to people who are older than me. Influence the way I speak, the things I believe, and the choice to keep returning to You, so I can be clean before You and others. There is no special age at which I become more trustworthy. I can be trustworthy today. I can be faithful right now. I can be clean—because of You. I want this to be something that I pursue every day of my life.

THINK ABOUT IT

How can you be the example God wants you
to be today? Who would you most like to
impact by being a godly example?

EXAMPLE

*Therefore be imitators of God, as beloved
children. And walk in love, as Christ
loved us and gave himself up for us.*
EPHESIANS 5:1–2 ESV

Dear God, because You are so much greater than me,
I sometimes think it's not necessary to try to live up
to Your expectations. It can be easy to think that I
just can't do it, so why try? But Your Word says I'm
to imitate You because I'm Your child. I'm supposed
to love others and be sacrificial in the way I help
others. I'll never be You, but that should not stop me
from choosing to live a life that lets others know I
want to be like You. You love me, You gave Yourself
for me, and You have given me an example to follow.
So help me follow. Maybe my obedience will lead
someone else to want to become part of Your family.

THINK ABOUT IT

*Why is imitating God so important as
a life goal? Who can help you most?
How has God helped you follow Him?*

DON'T DO THIS ON YOUR OWN

"They do not practice what they preach."
MATTHEW 23:3

Lord, Your son, Jesus, met religious leaders and was disappointed. They said the right words and did the things people expected them to do, but their hearts weren't in it. They said one thing and did something entirely different. They wanted to lead, but their hearts were far away from You. I don't want anyone to feel that I don't practice what I preach. I want my actions and words to match. I will fail, but I don't want to give up. I can't do this on my own, and when I try, I will become like those religious leaders who say the right words and live different lives. People notice when I live a lie. Help them notice when I live Your truth.

THINK ABOUT IT

Do you trust someone who lies to you? Why or why not? How is a failure to practice what you preach a lie? What would you need to change to get your words and actions to match?

WELL PLEASED

*Don't forget to do good and to share with those
in need. These are the sacrifices that please God.*
HEBREWS 13:16 NLT

Father, I would be foolish to decide to live a life that I knew did not please You. Whether I forget to make the right choices or intentionally make the wrong choices, please remind me as often as necessary that if I want to please You, I need to show Your love to the people You love. There should be no boundaries on my compassion, no exclusions, no question marks. You love all people, so help me love all people. Help me share with those in need. Help me to do things that benefit other people. You call this a sacrifice that pleases You. You have laws that every human being breaks, but that doesn't stop You from loving every human being. May You be my example.

THINK ABOUT IT

*Why do you think doing good and sharing
with others pleases God? Why do you think
the Bible calls these choices a sacrifice?*

LOOK UP

*If then you have been raised with Christ, seek the
things that are above, where Christ is, seated at the
right hand of God. Set your minds on things that
are above, not on things that are on earth.*
COLOSSIANS 3:1–2 ESV

Dear God, when I decided Your way was better than
mine, I also needed to decide that where You live is
where I want to be one day. What you think is most
important means that some of what I consider important is more like a game of trivia. Your ideas are
important and should be high on my priority list.
You care deeply about what I think, but You urge me
also to keep learning from You. Your ideas change
things for me, and I want things to change. I pray
that my thinking will be big enough to include You
and the home You're making for me.

THINK ABOUT IT

*What does "if then you have been raised with Christ"
mean? How should this change affect your decisions?*

SHARE IT

*I have not kept the good news of your justice hidden
in my heart; I have talked about your faithfulness and
saving power. I have told everyone in the great assembly
of your unfailing love and faithfulness. LORD, don't hold
back your tender mercies from me. Let your unfailing
love and faithfulness always protect me.*

PSALM 40:10–11 NLT

Lord, You use Your Word to show me what prayer
looks like. You make it clear that the Good News I
accepted is the same news that I should share. I
shouldn't hide it, or wait for someone to ask, and
telling many people is even better than telling a
few. You are faithful, You have the power to rescue,
Your love never fails, and I don't have to call in a
reservation for Your mercy. This is the best news of
the day. Help me share it.

THINK ABOUT IT

*How can hiding God's Good News help
others? What part of God's Good News
can you share today? Will you?*

THE SEARCH AND THE RESCUE

*Ye shall seek me, and find me, when ye
shall search for me with all your heart.*
JEREMIAH 29:13 KJV

Father, I need to be committed to seeking You, because You're committed to being found. The more investment I have in the search, the greater the joy in finding You. Faith gives me spiritual eyes to see something that I wasn't sure existed. You didn't say that I *might* find You if I seek for You. You said I *would* find You. You exist, and You want to be found. The discovery is mine to make. It's a personal discovery, and it's supposed to be. Maybe the reason some people can't seem to find You is because they're not looking for You. The search for You must be made with a heart willing to go the distance in the search. Give me that kind of heart.

THINK ABOUT IT

*Why do you think God wants to be found? Why do
you think He wants You to search for Him? How
does it make a difference when you want to search?*

NEW LIFE

*We have stopped evaluating others from a human
point of view. At one time we thought of Christ
merely from a human point of view. How differently
we know him now! This means that anyone who
belongs to Christ has become a new person.
The old life is gone; a new life has begun!*
2 CORINTHIANS 5:16–17 NLT

Lord, one of the ways I'm recognized as a newly-created believer is when I stop seeing other people the way I've always viewed them. When I know You for who You really are, I can see other people the way You see them. I no longer evaluate someone based of the way they look, where they live, or anything else that distracts me from the fact that they are created in Your image, and that You love them. My new life includes a need to let go of prejudice in favor of love.

THINK ABOUT IT

*Why is your willingness to look at people
differently a part of new-life living?
Not everyone can do this. Who can?*

NOT RESTORED, REPLACED

*You were taught, with regard to your former way of
life, to put off your old self, which is being corrupted
by its deceitful desires; to be made new in the attitude
of your minds; and to put on the new self, created to
be like God in true righteousness and holiness.*

Ephesians 4:22–24

Father, I can't take my old spiritual life and restore
it like a classic car. My old spiritual life was born to
die. I can trade this decaying life for the new life You
offer. This new life is radically different than the one
I traded in. It is built for impacting this world now
and preparing me for an eternity with You. New-life
living changes my mind, my choices, and my obedience. You make that possible. You take what I once
was and make Your new life fit me perfectly.

THINK ABOUT IT

*What are you supposed to do with your old life?
Why do you think God wants to give you a
new life and not just repair the old life?*

NO LONGER CONDEMNED

There is therefore now no condemnation for those who are in Christ Jesus. For the law of the Spirit of life has set you free in Christ Jesus from the law of sin and death. For God has done what the law, weakened by the flesh, could not do.
ROMANS 8:1–3 ESV

Dear God, new-life living means I'm no longer condemned. Your Son's payment on the cross can keep my sin account clean. You have set me free from a law that condemned and sentenced me. You did what my best effort never could. The sacrifice of Jesus on the cross paid for my sin. When I break Your rules, You no longer condemn me, You just want me to admit I've broken Your law and want to keep my God conversation going. When I think I'm condemned, help me remember that I'm Your child, and You're a great Dad.

THINK ABOUT IT

How does the word condemned *make you feel? Why is forgiveness better?*

FREEDOM

We know that our old sinful selves were crucified with Christ so that sin might lose its power in our lives. We are no longer slaves to sin. For when we died with Christ we were set free from the power of sin. And since we died with Christ, we know we will also live with him.
Romans 6:6–8 NLT

Lord, Your Son was put to death for my sin. He rose from the dead as the rescuer of mankind. My old life was put to death, and new-life living showed up in its place. New-life living makes me desire the freedom to live with greater wisdom, support, and goals. Each of these are empowered by You. If sin is a chain, you break it. If sin is a cloud, You bring out the sun. If sin is a trap, You remove it. With You, sin's power doesn't have to be a dictator.

THINK ABOUT IT

How can new-life living change relationships? What do you think being "set free from the power of sin" means?

THE WORDS I HEAR

Obscene stories, foolish talk, and coarse jokes—these are not for you. Instead, let there be thankfulness to God.
EPHESIANS 5:4 NLT

God, I'm familiar with locker-room talk. I can't seem to get away from dirty jokes. Guys will say things about girls that they would never say to those girls. I believe this is wrong, but I find myself laughing at what's being said. I can't always get away from it, but these things aren't for me. They don't promote new-life living. You give me so many good things to choose. You gave me a new life. You give me a way out when temptations show up without an invitation. Because I choose to love You and respect people, help me avoid allowing the words of others to influence the way I think about You and Your people. Thanks for the help.

THINK ABOUT IT

Why do you think God wants you to avoid obscene stories and foolish talk? Why do you think these things are not for you?

WHO I AM

*For by the grace given to me I say to everyone among
you not to think of himself more highly than he ought to
think, but to think with sober judgment, each according
to the measure of faith that God has assigned.*

ROMANS 12:3 ESV

Father, I have choices to make. My old thinking
made comparisons a test to prove whether I'm better or worse than other people. You tell me the only
true comparison is between Jesus and people. Jesus
never sinned, but people do. Jesus is always faithful, but people aren't. Jesus tells the truth, but people brag. So my response is to think of myself and
others correctly. We all need You, and no one is better or worse than another. I'm Your child. I'm loved.
I'm not perfect. I need forgiveness. Somewhere in
the middle, You found me. That's me—imperfect,
but found.

THINK ABOUT IT

*What does it mean to think highly of yourself?
What does it mean to have sober judgement?*

CHOICES MATTER

Should we keep on sinning so that God can show us more and more of his wonderful grace? Of course not! Since we have died to sin, how can we continue to live in it?

ROMANS 6:1–2 NLT

Dear God, Your grace is incredible. It invites me into Your family and pays for my sin. Grace gives me something I could never earn and never deserve. It could be easy for me to intentionally do the wrong thing because I know You'll forgive me. It's almost as if I'm telling You that I don't think Your grace has value. You've given me a way out when it comes to sin, so please stop me from playing a game of "How Many Times Can I Be Forgiven?" Don't get me wrong, I will need forgiveness. I just don't want to act as if my choices don't matter to You, because they do.

THINK ABOUT IT

Why should those with a new life in Christ die to sin? What do you think that means?

WORDS

*For the word of God is alive and active. Sharper
than any double-edged sword, it penetrates even
to dividing soul and spirit, joints and marrow;
it judges the thoughts and attitudes of the heart.*

HEBREWS 4:12

Lord, the words I read in the Bible aren't just thoughts
that only made sense when they were written. They
make sense today. They'll always make sense. Like
a sword, Your words separate fact from fiction. The
things I thought were true can be proven false when
they disagree with Your words. If Your words were a
spotlight, my thoughts and attitudes are exposed for
what they are. Nothing is hidden from You, and I can
learn what You think when I read Your words. You
call these words alive, active, sharp, and penetrating.
They are able to determine what I think. Your words
are powerful.

THINK ABOUT IT

*Why are God's words so important? How can
God's words help you understand what God wants
from you, and what God wants for you? How
should God's words change the way you think?*

LOVE'S INTRODUCTION

*Your unfailing love is better than life itself;
how I praise you! I will praise you as long as
I live, lifting up my hands to you in prayer.*
PSALM 63:3–4 NLT

Lord, because Your love is more valuable than life itself, let me accept, share, and praise You for Your love as long as I live. Really, it's as simple as that. You introduced love to this world when You made human beings. You wanted our lives to be dedicated to that same kind of love. When I choose to praise You, I am thanking You for Your love, and I'm showing love to You. I do this because I recognize how bad things would be if You withheld Your love. You guaranteed unfailing love and gave me prayer as a way to express how amazing I think You are.

THINK ABOUT IT

*Why do you think God's love is better than
your next breath? Why is praising God
a perfect reaction to His love?*

WHEN COMPARED

*Yes, everything else is worthless when compared with
the infinite value of knowing Christ Jesus my Lord.
For his sake I have discarded everything else,
counting it all as garbage, so that I could gain Christ.*
PHILIPPIANS 3:8 NLT

Father, what's worthless compared to knowing You?
Popularity? Yes. Video games? Yes. Sports? Yes.
Everything? I think I'm getting the point. The value
of knowing You is infinite. There's nothing I can
know, or do, or experience that will ever come close
to knowing You, Your Spirit, and Your Son. I have
to admit that if I'm given a choice between You and
something else, I will sometimes choose something
else. I'm sorry. Help me really see the difference
in the value of a relationship with You as superior
to the value of everything else. When other things
become more important than You, help me choose
what to get rid of.

THINK ABOUT IT

*What is everything else worth when compared
to Christ? For whose sake should you get
rid of everything else? Why?*

OUT OF STEP

Blessed is the one who does not walk in step with the wicked or stand in the way that sinners take or sit in the company of mockers, but whose delight is in the law of the Lord, and who meditates on his law day and night.

PSALM 1:1–2

Dear God, I'm blessed when I don't use the GPS of the wicked. I don't fall for people willing to help me sin, or decide to spend quality time with people who make fun of You. Sadly, these are easy things to do because I'm curious. Instead of trusting You, I want to learn for myself. I want to see if things are really as bad as You say. But I always come away from the experience convinced You were right. Because of Your grace, I can take pleasure in learning what pleases You. I can spend time learning about Your love and sharing it with others—the wicked, the sinners, and those who mock. You are my GPS. You give me direction.

THINK ABOUT IT

How can other people influence the choices you make? What can you do to counter what wickedness teaches?

THE FEAR BAN

There is no fear in love, but perfect love casts out fear. For fear has to do with punishment, and whoever fears has not been perfected in love. We love because he first loved us.
1 JOHN 4:18–19 ESV

Father, You loved me before I knew You. You loved me before I loved You. You loved me when I lived in rebellion. *You loved me.* When I understand that I can't change Your mind, and that You will always love me, I'm no longer afraid of You. I become totally in awe of You. Before I knew You, I only understood that You had a law and I broke it. Sin separated me from you, and all I could think of was the disappointment of my sin, not the unexpected gift of Your love. I knew I was guilty, but I didn't know how to be forgiven. Your love forgave me and saved me from my fear.

THINK ABOUT IT

Why are some people afraid of God?
Why don't Christians need to be afraid of God?

WEARABLE

*Since God chose you to be the holy people he loves,
you must clothe yourselves with tenderhearted mercy,
kindness, humility, gentleness, and patience.*
COLOSSIANS 3:12 NLT

Lord, You love me. You chose me. My best clothing comes from You. When someone hurts me, I wear mercy. When someone is rude to me, I wear kindness. When pride threatens to take over my closet, I wear humility. When life is brutal, I wear gentleness. When people irritate me or I'm in a hurry, I wear patience. This is the spiritual clothing of Your family. I'm one of many who are set apart from inferior garments like anger, jealousy, and hate. You chose me and gave me spiritual clothing for every occasion. Help me wear each garment with gratitude, knowing that if You didn't love me, my wardrobe would be very limited.

THINK ABOUT IT

*Which piece of spiritual clothing seems
the hardest to wear? Does it help to think of
these traits as clothing? Why or why not?*

SUPPLEMENTS

*Make every effort to supplement your faith with virtue, and
virtue with knowledge, and knowledge with self-control,
and self-control with steadfastness, and steadfastness
with godliness, and godliness with brotherly affection, and
brotherly affection with love. For if these qualities are yours
and are increasing, they keep you from being ineffective or
unfruitful in the knowledge of our Lord Jesus Christ.*
2 PETER 1:5–8 ESV

Dear God, some people take vitamins because they
believe they can help them gain better physical
health. But You offer spiritual vitamins that improve
my spiritual health. A trust vitamin goes well with
a dose of faithfulness. Regular use of knowledge
should be balanced with restraint. Dedication is a
companion to virtue. Devotion leads to comprehen-
sive love. Since love is Your greatest command, help
me follow Your plan to a life that starts with faith
and ends with love. These vitamins help keep me
healthy and strong for You.

THINK ABOUT IT

*Why should the qualities listed in these verses
continue growth in the life of a Christian? What
should be the outcome of following these traits?*

THE CHALLENGE OF ERROR

Brothers and sisters, if someone is caught in
a sin, you who live by the Spirit should restore
that person gently. But watch yourselves, or you
also may be tempted. Carry each other's burdens,
and in this way you will fulfill the law of Christ.

GALATIANS 6:1–2

Lord, when I recognize that someone broke Your law, why is it so easy for me to condemn them instead of offering help? One way I can help restore them is by loving them enough to tell them the truth about sin. I can help them see the wisdom in admitting their sin to You. But helping them can be challenging. I can be tempted to act like I'm better than they are, and I can question how important it really is to obey. But You ask me to help others, and when I do, I am obeying the God who helps me.

THINK ABOUT IT

In what ways can helping others see error
lead to temptation? What does the Bible mean
when it says to "carry each other's burdens"?

FAITH GLASSES

Faith shows the reality of what we hope for;
it is the evidence of things we cannot see....
By faith we understand that the entire universe
was formed at God's command, that what we now
see did not come from anything that can be seen.
HEBREWS 11:1, 3 NLT

Father, faith is like finally getting glasses when I've struggled to see. What I see with faith is so much more than what weak eyes think they see. Faith clears up what seemed to be unknowable. Even when I can't make sense of how the world was created, faith makes it clear that You were the one who made it. Faith means trusting that the things I can't understand are still explainable. The one who can explain it is You. The truth is I don't even need an explanation to believe You can be trusted. Faith lets regular people like me see You for who You are.

THINK ABOUT IT

Is faith wishful thinking or finally
seeing the truth? Why? How does faith
provide evidence of the unknown?

THE GOLDEN RULE

"In everything, do to others what you would have them do to you, for this sums up the Law and the Prophets."
MATTHEW 7:12

Dear God, if I wouldn't want someone to be mean to me, I shouldn't be mean. If I want someone to be friends with me, I should be a friend first. You tell me that I should pray for those I think of as enemies. You tell me I should forgive others for being mean. This verse shows me what to do before I even know how someone will treat me. If I treat people fairly, I'm honoring You and Your rules. If they don't treat me the same way, I should continue to treat them fairly. I don't need to guess. Your plan for relationships is the same before and after: *love*.

THINK ABOUT IT

Why is it so hard to be kind to someone who is not kind? Why is it so hard to forgive someone when they don't seem to care? Who has done this for You?

JOURNEY WISE

The LORD grants wisdom! From his mouth come knowledge and understanding. He grants a treasure of common sense to the honest. He is a shield to those who walk with integrity. He guards the paths of the just and protects those who are faithful to him.
PROVERBS 2:6–8 NLT

Father, this journey of the Christ follower has benefits I never expected. There are those who try to distract me from this journey, and they have arguments that sometimes make sense to me. What I learn from You is that they are wrong. You are the sole owner of wisdom, and You share it with Your family. If I listen closely, I can hear You share Your understanding. I have an account in Your common sense bank, and I can make withdrawals whenever needed. When I learn from Your wisdom and follow Your rules, You guard and protect me in this amazing journey.

THINK ABOUT IT

Why do you think the only source of wisdom is God? What three things have you learned about God's wisdom today?

PURE WISDOM

The wisdom that comes from heaven is first of all pure;
then peace-loving, considerate, submissive, full of mercy
and good fruit, impartial and sincere. Peacemakers
who sow in peace reap a harvest of righteousness.
JAMES 3:17–18

Lord, Your wisdom doesn't come with more than one set of rules. Wisdom seeks peace and is rewarded with right living. Wisdom doesn't seek to show off. Wisdom listens first before giving answers. It's humble, merciful, and mature. Wisdom doesn't take sides before hearing all sides. It is authentic and genuine. I'm not telling You anything You don't already know, but I think it's important to say that I'm learning, and I'd love to have Your wisdom teach me how to grow up. Help me see Your wisdom as the best way for me to learn from You, and the best way to remember that others need Your wisdom too.

THINK ABOUT IT

How does God's description of wisdom seem
different from what you thought? How can you
combine wisdom with being peace-loving?

RIGHT LIVING LESSONS

God's discipline is always good for us, so that
we might share in his holiness. No discipline is
enjoyable while it is happening—it's painful!
But afterward there will be a peaceful harvest of
right living for those who are trained in this way.
<small>HEBREWS 12:10–11 NLT</small>

Father, as long as I live, I will always be in training. I'll never know everything You can teach me. When You teach me a lesson and I flunk the test, help me understand that You have more than one way to instruct. Your discipline isn't a punishment, but a new direction in the learning process. I probably won't enjoy Your discipline, but I do want to share in Your plan. The plan that sets me apart for something You are preparing me to do. When I finally learn Your lessons, I'll be able to enjoy the right living You want for me.

THINK ABOUT IT

When are God's lessons most helpful? When
is God's discipline enjoyable? When can you
expect a peaceful harvest of right living?

REPRESENT

*Whatever you do, work heartily, as for the
Lord and not for men, knowing that from
the Lord you will receive the inheritance as
your reward. You are serving the Lord Christ.*
COLOSSIANS 3:23–24 ESV

Dear God, I will do a lot of different things in my life, and every time I do something at a job site, at home, or in school, help me treat each task as if it was something You asked me to do. I want my attitude to be right, my work ethic to be strong, and my determination to be unstoppable. Help me finish well. When I look at my work as something You pay attention to, I don't want to cut corners. I don't want to count the minutes until I can stop, or give up easily. I'm serving You more than I am working for someone else. Give me the strength to represent You well in my work.

THINK ABOUT IT

*How does your thinking change when you do
your work for God? Why should Christians
be thought of as excellent employees?*

SIN FEAR

People who conceal their sins will not prosper,
but if they confess and turn from them, they will
receive mercy. Blessed are those who fear to do wrong,
but the stubborn are headed for serious trouble.
PROVERBS 28:13–14 NLT

Father, I can't hide my sin from You. I'm not sure why I try to hide it. It's always best to admit when I've broken Your rules instead of pretending that I didn't. Help me turn my back on sin, so I can face You and accept Your forgiveness. Your Word says that I should be afraid to do wrong. I know I don't need to fear You, but to be afraid to sin means I really am equipped to obey You. I don't want to disappoint You. I don't need to fear Your forgiveness—I need to fear what sin does to stand in the way of my relationship with You. Help me fear sin because I love You.

THINK ABOUT IT

Why do you think God asks you to fear
doing wrong? Why does admitting
you've sinned often lead to mercy?

SAY WHAT?

With the tongue we praise our Lord and Father, and with it we curse human beings, who have been made in God's likeness. Out of the same mouth come praise and cursing. My brothers and sisters, this should not be.

JAMES 3:9–10

Lord, You created my tongue to speak words of praise. But I have used it to say things about people You've made. Those words can make You sad. I can say that I love You one minute and act like I don't know You the next minute. With my tongue I can express love and hate, peace and discontent, praise and cursing. None of these go well together. How can I disrespect others if I am to represent You? How can I talk about Your wonder and then say some of Your people aren't very wonderful? This was never how You wanted my tongue to speak. This isn't what I want to speak.

THINK ABOUT IT

Why is what you say a reflection of the God you follow? Why does God care so much about the words you speak?

DEFERRED ATTENTION

"Watch out! Don't do your good deeds publicly, to be admired by others, for you will lose the reward from your Father in heaven. When you give to someone in need, don't do as the hypocrites do—blowing trumpets in the synagogues and streets to call attention to their acts of charity! I tell you the truth, they have received all the reward they will ever get.... Give your gifts in private, and your Father, who sees everything, will reward you."
MATTHEW 6:1–2, 4 NLT

Father, when I brag about doing good, I'm not showing anyone love and I'm not honoring You. If I'm understanding the words in Your book well enough, all the things I do should be good because I love You and I am obeying Your rules. Wanting others to praise me for what I should be doing anyway changes the reason why I do what I do. Help me do the right thing—not for me but for You.

THINK ABOUT IT

Why is seeking recognition for good deeds opposed by God? Why is waiting for God's approval better than receiving approval from others today?

STRENGTH IN CONTENTMENT

*I have learned to be content whatever the circumstances.
I know what it is to be in need, and I know what it is to
have plenty. I have learned the secret of being content
in any and every situation, whether well fed or hungry,
whether living in plenty or in want. I can do all this
through him who gives me strength.*

PHILIPPIANS 4:11–13

Dear God, I want to be satisfied with Your answers
no matter the circumstances. When I'm in need, help
me know that You take care of me. When I have more
than enough, let me be grateful. Maybe the greatest
secret to contentment is trust. I believe You will take
care of me, and with Your help I will have everything
I need to do what needs to be done. With Your help,
I can be satisfied in the work I do. With Your help,
circumstances won't cause me to lose trust in You.

THINK ABOUT IT

*When should you be content? How can you be
content when you want more than you have?*

DESIRED OUTCOME

Always be joyful. Never stop praying.
Be thankful in all circumstances, for this is
God's will for you who belong to Christ Jesus.
1 THESSALONIANS 5:16–18 NLT

Lord, when I'm seeking Your will, I'm interested in knowing the greatest goals You have for my life. You must really care for me if You know me well enough to have a desired outcome for my life. You tell me I can take the first steps on this life plan by rejoicing always, praying continually, and being thankful no matter what. This is Your desire for those who follow Your Son. The desired outcome of my life includes Your plan. That plan includes Your involvement, and Your involvement means there will never be a better plan. Because you've blessed me, let me find reasons to be joyful, give me compassion to pray for others, and cause me to find gratitude in forgotten places—today.

THINK ABOUT IT

Does knowing that God has a desired plan for your
life change the way you live? Why or why not?

LIFE, BY DECREES

*The instructions of the Lord are perfect, reviving
the soul. The decrees of the Lord are trustworthy,
making wise the simple. The commandments of
the Lord are right, bringing joy to the heart. The
commands of the Lord are clear, giving insight for
living. Reverence for the Lord is pure, lasting forever.
The laws of the Lord are true; each one is fair.*
PSALM 19:7–9 NLT

Dear God, Your perfect instruction brings life to my
world. I can trust Your rules—they make me wise.
Your commands bring joy. My life path is illuminated by Your clear orders. My respect for You lasts
forever. Your laws define truth, and each one is honest and fair. And if it sounds like I'm repeating myself, it's only because I need to remember that You
have a reason for Your rules. They always make my
life better. They are always perfect.

THINK ABOUT IT

*Why do you think the writer of this psalm spent so
much time talking about the perfection of God's
rules? Why should that be important to you?*

WISDOM WITHDRAWAL

The one who has knowledge uses words with restraint, and whoever has understanding is even-tempered. Even fools are thought wise if they keep silent, and discerning if they hold their tongues.

<small>PROVERBS 17:27–28</small>

Father, You own the knowledge vault. When I don't make a wisdom withdrawal from You, I say things I regret. But You want me to use my mind and choose my words carefully. When I speak carefully, I can be calm, cool, and collected. People who are wise know that sometimes the best thing they can do is listen. When I listen, I learn, and I avoid saying something stupid. When I listen more than I speak, people pay more attention to the words I actually speak. I want Your wisdom to be heard in those words. I want to figure out the difference between helpful words and words with no value.

THINK ABOUT IT

Why do you think there are times in conversation when silence is the best response? Can you describe a recent conversation you had when you wish you had said less?

GROWING UP

Brothers, do not be children in your thinking.
Be infants in evil, but in your thinking be mature.
1 CORINTHIANS 14:20 ESV

Lord, was it so long ago I thought of myself as a child? Sometimes people still treat me that way. I have made mistakes that cause people to think I need to grow up. To be more responsible and make better choices. I want the thoughts that I think to grow up too. Just as I grow from a boy to a man, You want me to grow in my thinking and in my spiritual life. You don't want me to grow up choosing evil over good. I don't have to have a past filled with sin in order to accept You. I can come to You early and grow up in You. Keep me following You and not choosing those things You know will never help me.

THINK ABOUT IT

Why do you think God wants you to grow
up in your relationship with Him? What
do you think "be infants in evil" means?

SPIRITUAL WORKOUT

*We can rejoice, too, when we run into problems and trials,
for we know that they help us develop endurance. And
endurance develops strength of character, and character
strengthens our confident hope of salvation. And this
hope will not lead to disappointment. For we know how
dearly God loves us, because he has given us the Holy
Spirit to fill our hearts with his love.*

ROMANS 5:3–5 NLT

Father, in sports I'll workout, I'll sweat, and I'll wonder why life has to be so hard. You say that joy can be found in the problems I face. How? Trials produce endurance, which improves my character, and my improvement assures me that Your rescue plan will never disappoint. Your help leads me to the place where I find that Your love has been waiting for me. The place that makes me feel like I'm finally home.

THINK ABOUT IT

*What good things can come from the problems
you face? Why is it important to remember
that God loves you when trials show up?*

A WONDERFUL LIFE

Rid yourselves of all malice and all deceit, hypocrisy, envy, and slander of every kind. Like newborn babies, crave pure spiritual milk, so that by it you may grow up in your salvation, now that you have tasted that the Lord is good.

1 PETER 2:1–3

Dear God, thank You for making a list of things that can put a roadblock in my relationship with You, my family, and my friends. That list includes hostility, dishonesty, insincerity, wanting what others have, and saying things about other people that I know aren't true. You want me to experience a spiritual taste of how wonderful a life with You can be. Help me replace these roadblocks with gentleness, honesty, sincerity, sharing what I have, and encouraging others in the things that are true of them. You have rescued me. Help this young man grow up.

THINK ABOUT IT

From the list above, what would you most like to get rid of? Why do you think you need to grow up in your faith?

GOD SIGHTINGS

No one has ever seen God; if we love one another,
God abides in us and his love is perfected in us.
1 JOHN 4:12 ESV

Dear God, I have never seen you. No one I know has ever seen you. Your Word says plainly that, "No one has ever seen [You]." Faith allows me to believe You exist without seeing You. But here's one way people can see what You do in the lives of the faithful: You take up residence in the lives of Your followers, and the love we have for each other makes it possible for Your love to show up in our lives. Since You are love, people see me best when I let Your love reach through me and touch others. People can see You in me. I pray that I will be willing to let them see You.

THINK ABOUT IT

How can other people see God in you?
Why is it important that we keep
coming back to the subject of love?

GODLINESS TRAINING

"Physical training is good, but training for godliness is much better, promising benefits in this life and in the life to come." This is a trustworthy saying, and everyone should accept it.
1 TIMOTHY 4:8–9 NLT

Father, if I keep my body in shape, but not my soul, I may have an admirable look, but I miss out on the value of resembling You. If I excel in sports, I may have faith in fans who follow me, but I may have forgotten to follow You. If my heart is healthy physically, but not spiritually, I might feel fit in body, but not in soul. You have never been opposed to good health, but that only preserves the life I live here on earth. Your great spiritual benefits package insures me not only in the here and now, but in eternity with You. Godliness training is what You recommend. Help me trust the message.

THINK ABOUT IT

Do you see the benefits of physical training? Why do you think spiritual training is even more important? How can you improve this type of training?

ALLEGIANCE

In your hearts revere Christ as Lord. Always be prepared to give an answer to everyone who asks you to give the reason for the hope that you have. But do this with gentleness and respect.
1 PETER 3:15

Lord, You have the authority to ask me to do something and expect me to obey. Your will is always more important than mine. As I learn more about the things You want me to do, I can also learn more about how to answer someone when they ask why I do the things I do. I'm certain You're the only one who could ever rescue me. I'm certain You paid for my sins. I'm certain You offer forgiveness to those who serve You. Because I'm certain, help me be confident in respectfully sharing why pledging allegiance to You is the best choice anyone can make.

THINK ABOUT IT

Why do you think God wants you to be prepared to tell others about Him? Why is it important to show others respect when sharing with them?

ON PURPOSE

We urge you, brothers, admonish the idle, encourage the
fainthearted, help the weak, be patient with them all.
1 THESSALONIANS 5:14 ESV

Dear God, You made me on purpose. You've given me a purpose. But I can't do what you want me to do if I'm lazy, fearful, or weak. If that's true of me, it's true of everyone. I'm supposed to help those who struggle to take the first steps of faith, who feel anxious about what following might mean, and don't seem to have enough strength to move beyond where they find themselves today. My encouragement shouldn't sound like someone bossing others around, but like someone reminding others that You can help them take the next step. Instead of pointing out their weaknesses, help me remind them that Your strength is their strength. Then help me remember that there are times when I find myself lazy, fearful, and weak. I will always need Your help to stay strong.

THINK ABOUT IT

Why should you encourage people who struggle?
Why does God need to remind you to be patient?

INACTION

*Don't just listen to God's word. You must do what
it says. Otherwise, you are only fooling yourselves.
For if you listen to the word and don't obey, it is like
glancing at your face in a mirror. You see yourself,
walk away, and forget what you look like. But if you
look carefully into the perfect law that sets you free,
and if you do what it says and don't forget what you
heard, then God will bless you for doing it.*

JAMES 1:22–25 NLT

Father, what good is it for me to hear what you want
and then ignore what you ask? That would be like
having a parent asking me to clean my room, but my
choosing to play a video game or check status up-
dates on my phone as soon as they left. Forgetting
what they asked me to do would leave the room a
mess and my parent unhappy. Lord, I'm fooling myself if I think You're okay with that kind of response.

THINK ABOUT IT

*Why is listening to God's Word not enough?
Why is it so easy to forget what God asks?*

READ THE INSTRUCTIONS

"Study this Book of Instruction continually. Meditate on it day and night so you will be sure to obey everything written in it. Only then will you prosper and succeed in all you do."

JOSHUA 1:8 NLT

Lord, You have instructions for living, and I don't do myself any favors by never reading them. I can't live the best life without knowing how to live it. I can't honor You by acting as if the instructions are a waste of my time. You want me to think about it during the day and before I go to bed. I can't obey You if I don't know what You want me to do—and I can't do what You want me to do if I refuse to read and understand what You want. You have wisdom. I know where to find it. Give me the curiosity to read and the courage to obey.

THINK ABOUT IT

How often should you study God's book of instructions? How often should you think about it?

APPROVED

*Do your best to present yourself to God as
one approved, a worker who has no need to be
ashamed, rightly handling the word of truth.*
2 TIMOTHY 2:15 ESV

Dear God, if You were to ask me to think about how I have spent my time representing You, I don't know whether I would have Your stamp of approval. I might even feel ashamed that I've let so many other things come before You. I should give my best, but sometimes I don't give anything. Thanks for loving me enough to keep reminding me that a friendship with You is always worth my investment. You don't want me to live my life without knowing Your Word, sharing Your story, and believing Your truth. Help me learn to be able to use Your Word to tell others about this wonderful life.

THINK ABOUT IT

*Why should it be important to you that
God would approve of your choice to learn
from His Word? What choice could you
make that might leave you ashamed?*

CHANGELESS

Jesus Christ is the same yesterday, today, and forever.
So do not be attracted by strange, new ideas.
HEBREWS 13:8–9 NLT

Dear God, Your Son, Jesus, came to tell human beings how they could reconnect with You. He gave His life, won the war against death, and delivered Your great rescue plan. His message was consistent. His love was without challenge. His promise was unbreakable. The truth Jesus shared in the past is still true today. What I learn from God's Word today will still be true tomorrow. I don't need to consider new ways to believe, because I already believe in You. Truth can't change just because I don't like it. You don't change just because I think it would be better if You were something different. I can't make You into anything new. You are who You are. You don't change, and that's enough.

THINK ABOUT IT

Why should you find ideas that are different than
God's ideas unattractive? Why can you trust Jesus?
Why is it good news that Jesus is changeless?

IN TRAINING

Train up a child in the way he should go:
and when he is old, he will not depart from it.
PROVERBS 22:6 KJV

Lord, You want me to be trained in Your Word so I can follow in Your footsteps. You want me to understand Your instructions so I can reach the place where You're sending me. But I don't know what You know, and I will need Your help in understanding Your plan. The Bible is the perfect place for me to start, but I also need someone to help me learn. This could be an older family member, or someone at church. When I see an example of a person living a life that pleases You, I get some idea of how You want me to live. And if I have children of my own, someday You will help me train them in the way I am learning.

THINK ABOUT IT

Why should you want to be trained in living
for God? How does being trained help
you want to train others?

RESOLVED. RESCUED. REACHING.

*We are Christ's ambassadors; God is making
his appeal through us. We speak for Christ
when we plead, "Come back to God!"*
2 CORINTHIANS 5:20 NLT

Dear God, I represent You. I am an ambassador. You
have an invitation to a rescue that You want to share
with others. It's an invitation You want me to deliver.
There are benefits people need to know about. You
want people to resolve the differences between their
choice to sin and Your choice to forgive. This too is
something You've asked me to be a part of. Your appeal for people to come to You needs a voice, and
You want me to use mine. I can't imagine someone
who has the job of ambassador intentionally keeping Your Good News to themselves. You have a message that radically changes futures. May I never be
content to keep this Good News to myself.

THINK ABOUT IT

*What responsibilities do you think you have
as an ambassador of Christ? How can
you speak for Christ? Why should you?*

CHOSEN

You are a chosen people, a royal priesthood,
a holy nation, God's special possession, that
you may declare the praises of him who called
you out of darkness into his wonderful light.

1 PETER 2:9

Father, Your Word is my best encouragement. Thank You. In Your book, I discover I'm chosen by You to be part of Your royal family. I'm part of a nation set apart as Your special possession. It means so much that You want me to be a part of Your nation. I'm not an afterthought, and I'm not on a quest to win Your love because it was Your love that made me valuable to You. When I pay attention to all the things You have done for me, I want to praise You. I want to tell others about Your greatness, and explain how a life known for darkness can shine with new light when that life accepts the truth—that they are chosen, set apart, and can become members of Your family.

THINK ABOUT IT

How does it feel to know God chose you?
How does being wanted lead to gratitude?

UNEXPECTED BLESSINGS

*"God blesses those who are poor and realize
their need for him, for the Kingdom of Heaven
is theirs. God blesses those who mourn, for they
will be comforted. God blesses those who are
humble, for they will inherit the whole earth."*
MATTHEW 5:3–5 NLT

Father, You are the God who blesses. If I think Your blessings only arrive in the stuff I can own or in money to purchase things, I don't really understand Your blessing. How can I think You mean money when You tell me I'm blessed when I don't have much? When I have a need, and I can't take care of it, it's much easier to believe You're the only One who can. But You tell me that trouble comes to everyone. So when those moments make me sad, I need to remember that You will comfort me and give me peace. I have more than I ever needed when I have You.

THINK ABOUT IT

*Why do you think realizing you need
God is a blessing? Why is sadness
a pathway to God's blessing?*

BLESSED BY BLESSING

"God blesses those who hunger and thirst for justice, for they will be satisfied. God blesses those who are merciful, for they will be shown mercy."
MATTHEW 5:6–7 NLT

Dear God, You bless me when I seek to help those who have been treated unfairly. You bless me when I show mercy to others, because mercy is usually returned. Life is hard, but as one of Your children I should do my best to show others what it looks like to be kind, helpful, and forgiving. Maybe I'm blessed with friendships, I have a good reputation, and I am treated kindly, but whatever the blessing looks like, it only comes when I learn how You want me to relate to other people. When I help others, I'm not only obeying You—I am catching a glimpse of what You've done for me every day of my life. Do I feel blessed? I do.

THINK ABOUT IT

What do you think it might look like to seek justice for someone else? Why is mercy something you should share?

GOD BLESSES

"God blesses those whose hearts are pure, for they will see God. God blesses those who work for peace, for they will be called the children of God. God blesses those who are persecuted for doing right, for the Kingdom of Heaven is theirs."
MATTHEW 5:8–10 NLT

Lord, when my mind and heart are in line with Your plan, when my choices live by Your rules, and when my soul is restored by Your forgiveness, I catch a glimpse of who You are, and it is satisfying. When I choose peace over fear and hatred, I gain the reputation that I am a member of Your family. When people pick on me because they don't understand You, I can remember I have access to You now, and I will be with You in the future. Your blessings often arrive in the disguise of difficulties. Help me wear this new life with joy because no matter what happens, I'm blessed.

THINK ABOUT IT

Why do you think God wants you to work for peace? Have you ever been picked on for doing the right thing? If so, what happened?

NOT ALONE

"God blesses you when people mock you and persecute you and lie about you and say all sorts of evil things against you because you are my followers. Be happy about it! Be very glad! For a great reward awaits you in heaven. And remember, the ancient prophets were persecuted in the same way."
MATTHEW 5:11–12 NLT

Dear God, I don't like to be picked on for following You, but it happens. I will need Your reassurance that You stand with me and will never abandon me. Help me remember that anything I face because of You is small in comparison to the blessing of knowing You, and of loving others because You loved first. People will say things that aren't true, but You say I'm part of Your family—and I will have a place in heaven where no one is picked on. I will be happy. I will be glad.

THINK ABOUT IT

Why is it so hard to accept the lies people say about you? What would cause you to be glad when someone picks on you?

TREASURE

*"Do not lay up for yourselves treasures on earth,
where moth and rust destroy and where thieves break
in and steal, but lay up for yourselves treasures in
heaven, where neither moth nor rust destroys and
where thieves do not break in and steal. For where
your treasure is, there your heart will be also."*
MATTHEW 6:19–21 ESV

Father, my greatest treasures are being saved for eternity. Why, then, do I keep thinking that the things I can hold on to today are more important? These treasures will decay. Rust will destroy them. People who also think these things are important can steal what I thought was so important. Heaven, the place my heart longs to be, is a place where what I have can never be stolen, where what's important will never decay, and what's of real value can never be destroyed. Thanks for giving and taking care of my greatest treasure.

THINK ABOUT IT

*What are three things you own and treasure?
Why are these things of less value than
what waits in heaven?*

THE CHOICE TO RETURN

Let the words of my mouth, and the meditation
of my heart, be acceptable in thy sight,
O LORD, my strength, and my redeemer.
PSALM 19:14 KJV

Dear God, I speak. I think. I consider. Sometimes the words and the thoughts aren't pleasing to me, and I have a sense that they don't please You. But I want them to. I want my words to match Your heart. I want my thoughts and conclusions to honor You. I will fail. I will say things I instantly regret. I will think things that surprise me. But in the end, help me return to You, to reset my thinking and allow You to recalibrate my heart. You have the strength I need, and You can restore my thoughts to Your perfect design. I pray you will do what needs to be done to change what I say and think to be in line with what You have said and thought.

THINK ABOUT IT

Why should you care about your words and
thoughts? Why is it important to remember
that your strength comes from God?

TAKING CARE

Then God said, "Let us make human beings in
our image, to be like us. They will reign over the
fish in the sea, the birds in the sky, the livestock,
all the wild animals on the earth, and the small
animals that scurry along the ground."
GENESIS 1:26 NLT

Lord, I was designed to be like You in the way I think
and speak. When earth's first family sinned, every
human ever born followed their example. In the beginning You gave mankind the job of looking after
the sea, sky, and land. Likewise, I'm supposed to
represent You in the way this world is taken care of.
You didn't give it to us to trash. Like any resource,
I should do my best to protect the earth as one
who is grateful for Your creation. I can't save this
planet—only You can do that. But help me be responsible with how I care for all the gifts of Your
creation.

THINK ABOUT IT

Is it important to represent God in the way
you take care of nature? Can you love God
and take care of His creation? Why or why not?

ONE BAD TRADE

They traded the truth about God for a lie. So they worshiped and served the things God created instead of the Creator himself, who is worthy of eternal praise! Amen.
ROMANS 1:25 NLT

Father, You made this planet for me to enjoy, not to worship. No matter how much beauty I discover in nature, it's something You created, but it's not You. The Bible tells me about a time when people were in the mood to trade. They traded Your truth for a promise that would never come true. People worshiped the earth and the things You created, but they totally forgot You. They loved what You made, but they acted as if You'd never created anything. They should have offered You praise, but they gave Your creation a parade. They gave the earth the most dignified honor. Help me see the beauty of this world—then remember that You made it.

THINK ABOUT IT

Why do you think the Bible says it's a lie to believe the earth is to be worshipped? Why should God always be worshipped above all?

HIS NAME

"You shall not misuse the name of the
Lord your God, for the Lord will not hold
anyone guiltless who misuses his name."
EXODUS 20:7

Dear God, You created everything. I can grow a flower because You created flowers. I can climb a mountain because You made the rocks, the dirt and the trees. You're awesome. This is true, and I know it's true, but there are times when I don't treat Your name with respect. There are times I'm more impressed by what You've made than by You. The way I say Your name tells other people how I really feel about You. When I misuse Your name, I don't show respect. Others will believe the tone of my voice more than the words I use to describe Your love. If I don't respect my parents, people notice. Why should it be any different with You? Help me show You honor by being careful to respect Your name.

THINK ABOUT IT

Have you been challenged to rethink the way
you show respect to God's name? In what ways?

BIG PLANS

*Let us not grow weary of doing good, for in due
season we will reap, if we do not give up. So then, as
we have opportunity, let us do good to everyone, and
especially to those who are of the household of faith.*
GALATIANS 6:9–10 ESV

Lord, I have choices to make. I could do something that honors You, but it might be more effort than I want to give. I could do something that's easy, but it refuses to make Your name famous. You have big plans for the world that I live in, and I don't want to stand in the way. More than that, I want to help in any way You ask. When You give me an opportunity to do something that shows Your goodness, let me take it. Let me champion Your cause and refuse to give up.

THINK ABOUT IT

*When you follow God, why is it important not to give
up? Have you ever thought of God as someone who
gives you opportunities to do big things for Him?*

RUN FREE

*Since we are surrounded by such a huge crowd
of witnesses to the life of faith, let us strip off
every weight that slows us down, especially the
sin that so easily trips us up. And let us run with
endurance the race God has set before us.*
HEBREWS 12:1 NLT

Dear God, I would never want to run a race with a fifty-pound backpack resting on my shoulders, but sometimes I feel like I'm carrying a burden that prevents me from seeing where I need to go. Help me give You everything that slows me down. You have agreed to take what I don't need. All I really need is You. Take my backpack of sin, my satchel of fear, and my suitcase of pain. Help me run Your race with freedom and hope. Help me endure each step and look forward to the finish line.

THINK ABOUT IT

*Is it important to be an example of what
freedom in Christ looks like? Why or why not?*

WON

*We do this by keeping our eyes on Jesus,
the champion who initiates and perfects our
faith. Because of the joy awaiting him, he endured
the cross, disregarding its shame. Now he is seated
in the place of honor beside God's throne.*

HEBREWS 12:2 NLT

Father, I can run the race and give You my burdens when I focus on Your Son, Jesus. He has run the race I'm on and He relied on You. So when I focus on Jesus, the Champion, my faith is made stronger. He was able to understand the race because He faced the cross and won. He could have felt shame, but He was thinking of me, and of how much I would need rescue. Jesus won His race, and now He lives with You. Keep fine-tuning my faith. Keep my attention on You, and welcome me home at the end of my race.

THINK ABOUT IT

*Why is it important to keep your focus on Jesus?
Why is Jesus' example so valuable to your race?*

DIFFICULT

Think of all the hostility [Jesus] endured from sinful
people; then you won't become weary and give up.
HEBREWS 12:3 NLT

Lord, it's easy to think I'm the only one who's ever
faced struggles. It really seems that way when I'm
going through something I feel like no one could
understand. I even convince myself that You have
no idea how hard things are. Of course that's ridic-
ulous, but on my hardest days I feel alone. Your Son
knows. He understands. The hostility of people who
didn't care interfered with His mission all the time.
He faced struggles I never will. Help me remember
that I can endure the hardest days, and that I never
face them alone. I don't want to give up, even when I
am tired of the problems I encounter. Walk with me
and give me the strength I need to do hard things
with Your help.

THINK ABOUT IT

Why is it meaningful to remember that
Jesus wasn't always popular? How can
His example help you keep going?

PRESSURE RELIEF

*Blessed is the one who perseveres under trial because,
having stood the test, that person will receive the crown
of life that the Lord has promised to those who love him.*
JAMES 1:12

Father, Your plan for me is better than my best ideas.
You give me Your Word so I can understand Your
plan. But I will feel pressure to do something that
is not part of Your plan—maybe even today. That's
when I make a choice. I can either follow You, or I
can take a few steps away from Your plan. Help me
stand up to the pressure. Help keep my feet pointed
in Your direction. To obey You is to love You the way
You deserve to be loved. When the pressure comes,
remind me that You offer relief. Help me ask. Help
me say thanks.

THINK ABOUT IT

*Why would it be dangerous to think that you can
personally handle pressure from people who don't
love God? Why do you think God calls this a test?*

THE SHEPHERD

The Lord is my shepherd, I lack nothing.
PSALM 23:1

Dear God, I'm a sheep. That's what You call me. Sheep are not smart. Sheep are not strong. Sheep need help. I too need wisdom. I too need strength. I too need help. Yes, I am a sheep. That makes sense because You are my shepherd. You lead me, and I am wise if I follow. You teach me, and I am wise if I listen. You're willing to help, and I am wise if I accept. When I know that I need You, and I allow You to help, I lack nothing. I am part of Your flock. We are part of Your family. You are our shepherd, and You are also my shepherd. You care for us. You care for me. You are a good shepherd. Help me understand what You want me to do.

THINK ABOUT IT

What are some reasons you think God calls you a sheep? Why is God, the shepherd, worth following?

REFRESHED, RESTORED, REVIVED

He makes me lie down in green pastures, he leads me
beside quiet waters, he refreshes my soul. He guides
me along the right paths for his name's sake.
PSALM 23:2–3

Lord, when I need rest, You calm my spirit. When I'm thirsty, I can depend on You to satisfy my thirst. When my soul needs refreshing, You revive my soul. When I'm lost, You find me. You're the best guide. You do this because You love me. You do this because Your name should make me remember Your care. Your name invites me to trust You when I'm upset, to long for You, to need refreshing when I have lost my way. Your sheep struggle with these things. When I read about what You do for me, I feel taken care of. I feel loved. I feel grateful.

THINK ABOUT IT

How does it make you feel to know that God takes care of you? Why should God's name cause you to think of the word *trustworthy*?

THROUGH DARKNESS

Even though I walk through the darkest valley,
I will fear no evil, for you are with me;
your rod and your staff, they comfort me.
PSALM 23:4

Father, sometimes I feel like I walk into certain situations blindly. All I seem to see is darkness. But all I want to see is light. It feels like anything that could happen to me would be bad. Anything good would feel like a miracle. I need a miracle. When You walk with me, I have nothing to fear—and You always walk with me. You bring comfort in those moments when I am unsure, unsettled, and misunderstood. You have said that Your Word lights each new step because when I read Your Word, I can see where to go next. Keep me seeking Your direction, and help me be willing to walk in the direction that leads me out of every dark moment.

THINK ABOUT IT

Why should Christians refuse to fear evil? Why are difficult days a great opportunity to trust God?

EXPECTATIONS EXCEEDED

You prepare a table before me in the
presence of my enemies. You anoint
my head with oil; my cup overflows.
PSALM 23:5

Dear God, when it seems like I'm surrounded by people who don't want me to succeed, You make sure I'm spiritually fed. I will need the strength. My enemies want to see me fail, and they believe I will fail. But You want to see me succeed. You ask me to pay attention to You and not to the enemy of my soul. You make sure I know that I'm Your child, You are trustworthy, and there's no enemy that can win against You. When I read that my cup overflows, I have to believe that You provide more than enough for my needs. You offer more satisfaction than I ever expected. You go above and beyond what I ask and think.

THINK ABOUT IT

Does God fear any enemy? Why or why not?
What does it mean to have a cup that overflows?
How has God shown you He can be trusted?

THAT'S GOOD. THAT'S LOVE.

*Surely your goodness and love will follow
me all the days of my life, and I will
dwell in the house of the LORD forever.*
PSALM 23:6

Lord, You take care of me, and that's good. You rescued me, and that's love. You promised to never leave or abandon me, and this goodness and love will be part of my walk with You. There will never be a day when You call in sick or take a vacation. There will never be a time when You are just too weary to care. Your goodness and love always arrive with each new day's journey. I'm never without it. I always need it. I will be with You today because You are with me always. We are together. That's good. That's love. That's perfect.

THINK ABOUT IT

*How should you feel knowing that God's
goodness and love can be part of your life
today, tomorrow, and forever? How do you
feel knowing that God is always with you?*

FOR ME

We can confidently say, "The Lord is my helper;
I will not fear; what can man do to me?"
HEBREWS 13:6 ESV

Father, I can be bold, and I want to be. I can be brave,
and I need to be. I can be courageous, and You want
me to be. When I understand that You are in total
control of every personal encounter, I can be confident that even when I don't understand Your solution that solution is perfect. You have offered me
Your personal help, and I accept it. There is abso-
lutely nothing that any human can do to distance me
from Your love. There are no choices someone else
can make that will change Your mind about me. You
love me. You help me. And I can say boldly, bravely,
and courageously, "I will not fear."

THINK ABOUT IT

How does knowing the Lord as your helper improve
your confidence? How does knowing God can
take care of everything diminish your fear?

INSIDE WORK

Create in me a pure heart, O God,
and renew a steadfast spirit within me.
PSALM 51:10

Dear God, all the trying in the world won't make me pure. All my best efforts only prove that I can't please You on my own. All my worry over what I've done wrong just keeps me from asking You for help. I want a pure heart, but You'll have to create one within me. A faithful, steadfast spirit is something I want too, but I can't buy it, earn it, or trade for it. If change is going to happen in me, it will happen because I let You change me—not because I tried really hard to change myself. You want to make me new, and I need to get out of Your way.

THINK ABOUT IT

Who can create a pure heart and faithful
spirit within you? Why should you let Him?

MADE RIGHT

"A person is made right with God by faith in Jesus Christ, not by obeying the law. And we have believed in Christ Jesus, so that we might be made right with God because of our faith in Christ, not because we have obeyed the law. For no one will ever be made right with God by obeying the law."

GALATIANS 2:16 NLT

Lord, if I could obey every rule in Your book, I might be so proud of my accomplishment that I would tell everyone how good a person I am. If I could do the hard work of recording a perfect record in Your book, I wouldn't need You. Everyone sins. Jesus was the only perfect sacrifice for people who sin. I need You, and I know I will never have a perfect record through my own effort. My faith in Your Son is the only thing that will ever make things right with You.

THINK ABOUT IT

Making the right choice is important. What is the only choice that makes things right with God?

IMPERFECT AND LOVED

Blessed be God, because he has not rejected my
prayer or removed his steadfast love from me!
PSALM 66:20 ESV

Father, when I pray to You, I'm imperfect. This could stop me from praying, but You make sure it doesn't need to. Your love keeps reaching out to people who fail. My prayers are heard because You're good, not because I'm likable. Your love is relentless, faithful, and steadfast. Nothing I say or do will make You love me less. You want to hear what I say, and You want me to accept what You offer. You're a blessing, Lord, because Your love reaches into my imperfect heart. I know it's okay to talk to You. So once again, I'm here. Thanks for listening.

THINK ABOUT IT

Do you trust God more, or less, because
He promises to listen to your prayer and to
never stop loving you? Why? If prayer is
a conversation, how do you hear God?

FAILURE TO ASK

You do not have because you do not ask God.
When you ask, you do not receive, because
you ask with wrong motives, that you may
spend what you get on your pleasures.
JAMES 4:2–3

Dear God, I want things, so I do what I can to earn them. That might mean working when I want a new phone, a video game, or maybe even a car, but it doesn't work when the things I want require a change in my heart or someone else's. It doesn't work when circumstances are completely out of my control because I *didn't* ask for Your help. When I ask for things because I'm greedy or selfish, I can't expect You to give me what I want. When I know You best, I will ask for the thing that You're most passionate about.

THINK ABOUT IT

Why is it so hard to get what you want when
you don't ask God? What are some of the
reasons God might tell you "No"?

SHOW AND TELL

*Whatever you do or say, do it as a representative of the
Lord Jesus, giving thanks through him to God the Father.*
COLOSSIANS 3:17 NLT

Lord, I'll say things that bring honor to Your name,
but I'll also say things I regret. I'll do things that
represent who You are, but I'll also do things that are
a reflection of the sin in my life. I need to remember
that my life was reclaimed from the grip of sin when
I began my journey with Jesus. People will get an
introduction to You through my life. I know I'll never
be perfect, but I want to allow You to give me the
opportunity to represent You. . .and then help me
stand for You. May people see enough of You in my
imperfect life that they'll want to know You more.
Give me the words and show me the way to represent You well.

THINK ABOUT IT

*Why is being a part-time Christian never a good
way to live? Why does God want you to choose to
represent Him in all you show and all you tell?*

STAND STRONG

Be watchful, stand firm in the faith,
act like men, be strong.
1 CORINTHIANS 16:13 ESV

Father, there are men and women who become soldiers. They understand the rules a soldier follows.
They act like soldiers, they become strong both physically and mentally, and they learn to watch for the
enemy. This might be a picture of how You want me
to view my journey with You. There are things that
interfere with my choice to follow You. When I'm not
paying attention, my enemy will try to convince me
that there are things more important than faith, and
if I trust this message, I may stop making choices
that a Christian should make. Any spiritual strength
I might have diminishes as I become less interested
in following You. Help me identify the enemy and
stand strong in my faith. Help me act like Your
child and allow Your strength to keep me strong.

THINK ABOUT IT

How can you be both watchful and strong in your
faith? Why should you act like a child of God?

A BETTER PEACE

*[Jesus said], "I am leaving you with a gift—peace of
mind and heart. And the peace I give is a gift the
world cannot give. So don't be troubled or afraid."*
JOHN 14:27 NLT

Dear God, peace is a gift You give to Your family.
This peace doesn't mean I will never face trouble. It
means You know my situation and can take care of
all the details. I don't want to get caught up in trying
to make sense of things, and then miss out on Your
gift of peace. I don't need to be anxious. I shouldn't
be afraid. I will trust You. I will accept Your gift of
peace.

THINK ABOUT IT

*Why do you think God called peace a gift? Why is
God's peace different than other types of peace?*

WINNING CONNECTION

We are more than conquerors through him who loved us.
For I am convinced that neither death nor life, neither
angels nor demons, neither the present nor the future,
nor any powers, neither height nor depth, nor anything
else in all creation, will be able to separate us from the
love of God that is in Christ Jesus our Lord.

ROMANS 8:37–39

Lord, when I followed You, I joined the winning team. Before I followed You, death seemed frightening. The future was unknown, and I had so many things to fear. I needed You, but I was separated from You because I hadn't accepted Your gift of rescue. Now I am convinced that I win because there is nothing that can come between You and me. I have accepted Your love, and that's the best win of my life. Your love is amazing. It means I can be with You forever.

THINK ABOUT IT

Is it easy to believe that Christians are
the winning team? Why or why not?
What can separate you from God's love?

MORE THAN EXPECTED

*God is so rich in mercy, and he loved us so much, that
even though we were dead because of our sins, he gave
us life when he raised Christ from the dead. (It is only by
God's grace that you have been saved!)*
<small>EPHESIANS 2:4–5 NLT</small>

Father, it's become clear that You loved me more
than I could have expected. I have also learned that
my response should always be one of gratitude. Your
mercy reached out to me in ways I never deserved.
Your grace made me part of Your family. My faith
took my will and made Your plan more important.
I have discovered real life in this place where You
live, and as I follow You, I can see that my life is so
much better with You than it ever was without. Keep
leading me, because I want to keep following. Where
You're going is the place I've always needed to be.

THINK ABOUT IT

*Where does real life come from? Where does
real love come from? Why is it important
that the answer is the same?*

SCRIPTURE INDEX